Ace against Odds

Ace against Odds

SANIA MIRZA

with

IMRAN MIRZA AND SHIVANI GUPTA

Harper
Sport

First published in hardback in India in 2016 by Harper Sport
An imprint of HarperCollins *Publishers*

P-ISBN: 978-93-5136-263-0
E-ISBN: 978-93-5136-264-7

2 4 6 8 10 9 7 5 3 1

HarperCollins *Publishers*
A-75, Sector 57, Noida, Uttar Pradesh 201301, India
1 London Bridge Street, London, SE1 9GF, United Kingdom
Hazelton Lanes, 55 Avenue Road, Suite 2900, Toronto, Ontario M5R 3L2
and 1995 Markham Road, Scarborough, Ontario M1B 5M8, Canada
25 Ryde Road, Pymble, Sydney, NSW 2073, Australia
195 Broadway, New York, NY 10007, USA

Typeset in 11/14.5 Minion Pro at
SÜRYA, New Delhi

Printed and bound at
Replika Press (Pvt) Ltd.

CONTENTS

FOREWORD

As a severe dust storm raged through the city of Doha in February 2015, Sania and I practised together for the first time, and the memory is still fresh in my mind as though it was just yesterday. The session turned out to be disastrous and entirely forgettable. We were both so bad in that practice.

But I want to take you back to the first serious two-hour long conversation that Sania and I had a few days before we practised in Doha. In the course of our talk, I found myself inspired by Sania's intense desire to succeed. She seemed so determined to win, it was almost scary, even though most of the time we didn't even discuss our doubles game or what we wanted to achieve.

That evening, we talked about the singles match in which we played each other for the first time, in Dubai. I had heard about this young Indian girl who had beaten Svetlana Kuznetsova – the reigning US Open champion at the time (2005). So, the following year, after I had made my comeback, when I was drawn to play against this young, feisty Indian competitor named Sania Mirza, I took the duel very seriously. And for good reason. She possessed a deadly forehand which I tried to stay away from as far as possible. I won that match against her in Dubai, but over the years we ended up with an even 2-2 head-to-head lifetime singles record. I beat Sania in Dubai and Kolkata and she defeated me in Seoul and Los Angeles.

I am mentioning all this because we still see ourselves very much as singles players. The technique and strategy in tennis keeps changing, and in today's doubles, it is the all-round game that works best. Sania and I have been able to dominate only because we are able to hold our ground from the baseline and at the net against the current top-ranked players – singles or doubles. This is also where strategy and some thinking come in handy. I think we also score over our opponents with our temperament as we both love to embrace pressure situations. On many occasions it comes down to two or three crucial points in a match where you need nerves of steel. The 2015 Wimbledon final was a perfect example of what we can achieve under pressure: at one stage we looked entirely down and out!

Let me try to explain our 'phenomenon' Sania, whose tennis I think is magical, almost mystical. It is a fact that for a long time she has been one of the best doubles players in the world. It is also a fact that she has the best forehand out of three billion women on this planet!

As for me, I started playing doubles when I couldn't even see over the net and the racket bag was taller than me. I had to earn my spot to play with my best friend at the time. If I missed even a single ball, she would never play with me again – and that was pressure! Also, it was a simple education. For I wanted to play with the older kids like my life depended on it.

It was only logical then that I chose tall, powerful partners throughout my career. Like Sania. She has a merciless forehand and her well-placed serve starts us perfectly in each point. And this is not everything. She creates angles on returns that do not exist. Where other people would break their bones, she calmly produces winners with an incredible flick of the wrist.

As a team, we have come a long way since we had our first hit together in Doha. Neither of us is a practice champion, although I tried really hard because expectations were high. The one thing we had in common from the start was the belief in our abilities when it mattered. We both grow with the momentum and rise to the occasion under pressure. That is a gift and only champions are blessed with it. Sania surely has it.

Our partnership seems to have been made in heaven and maybe it was destiny that brought us together. We take a lot of pride in each other's achievements and when Sania became World No. 1 in Charleston for the first time, I was as excited as she was.

We continue to improve and make each other better every day. On a given day you may see one of us not at her best, but you will rarely find both of us not playing well. We are able to overturn impossible situations because of the immense trust we have in each other. Sania's positive energy and great attitude are gigantic contributions in every match.

I am happy and honoured to call her my partner and a friend for life.

MARTINA HINGIS

INTRODUCTION

Every once in a while, the universe throws up an anomaly in the context of Indian sport. In my opinion, to call Sania an anomaly is an understatement. I won't go into all the reasons why I believe so, as most of you already know them and that's why you are reading this book.

I have known Sania for close to fifteen years now and besides being a close friend of hers, I have been lucky enough to share the tennis court with her, resulting in a couple of Grand Slam titles for both of us.

When I was asked to write the introduction to her autobiography, I knew it would be a challenge, to encapsulate a fifteen-year relationship inclusive of all kinds of emotions.

When I first met Sania she was about fourteen years old. I hadn't interacted with her much but had heard from my dad that she had enough talent and firepower for us tennis lovers to be excited about. So we signed her up to help manage her career. Very soon, she translated that firepower into a Junior Wimbledon title as a baby-faced sixteen-year-old. This win was a first for Indian tennis, it galvanised both the sports fraternity in India and the tennis world globally. Here was a girl from a third-world country, well spoken, good-looking, and from a community that had almost never encouraged girls to take to sport. She had the perfect mix to become a star as long as she delivered results on the tennis court.

Two years later, Sania made her breakthrough in the women's game with a run at the Australian Open, and since then she has had a remarkable career. She has been, and continues to be, the face of some of the biggest brands in the country. She started off as the lone

Indian competing in the singles of the Grand Slams and continuously won rounds and pushed the contenders, until today, she sits on top of the women's doubles rankings comfortably, even threatening to fly past my Grand Slam tally in the near future.

To be singled out as special in life, one has to go through trials and tribulations. Sania has had more than her fair share, whether it was the fatwa against her, the surgeries she had to undergo, the constant public scrutiny of her personal life or just random folks asking why she had to play tennis wearing a skirt. She has always faced adversity with the same principles her life is built upon – single-minded focus, self-belief and self-respect. I believe she has been instrumental in changing the face of Indian sport, especially where women are concerned. Time will surely prove that. But in the meantime, we need to applaud how comprehensively she has made her mark in arguably the most popular individual sport in the world and the manner in which she continues to be India's ambassador on the global stage.

Enjoy the book!

MAHESH BHUPATHI

PROLOGUE

MY LEGS FELT heavy, my arms were numb. I could see the blurry tennis ball as it crossed the net and hit the surface of the court.

Fault. Just missed the line.

A few seconds more and the match was over, the tournament done and dusted. Casey Dellacqua had just served a double fault and I had won the biggest prize of my tennis career. The victory signalled my elevation as the 'numero uno' women's doubles player in the world – the culmination of a cherished dream!

As the chair umpire called 'game, set and match', my partner Martina Hingis ran towards me with a radiant smile, her right forefinger up in the 'No. 1' sign, and hugged me. That was when she revealed to me that it was here in this same tournament in 1997 that she had become the No. 1 player in the world for the first time – the youngest ever to have achieved that distinction.

The story of my entire career flashed before me as I struggled to come to terms with the seemingly unreal landmark I had just reached. Everything from depressing injuries and surgeries, to waking up early in the mornings, taking autorickshaw rides to reach the court, practising eight hours a day, getting massages and treatments for the nagging pains in my body, the sheer thrill of winning and the utter disappointment of losing – all these images flashed before my eyes. It was like a mini-movie playing out in front of me.

As I sat on a chair, waiting for the prize distribution ceremony to start, I barely had a few minutes to collect my thoughts. There was a complete sense of satisfaction, a kind of jubilation I had never felt before. It was a feeling that can never be matched or accurately described, no matter how often I continue to win. To have finally achieved the dream harboured for two decades was incredible. It felt surreal to be one of those lucky few who get to the mark they set for themselves as children. The odds had been stacked literally one in a billion against me. So much had to fall into place.

I knew that my career, in totality, would have been satisfactory even without this achievement of being officially acknowledged as the best doubles tennis player in the world, but being number two was never the goal. That I stayed in that exalted position for a considerable length of time, in the phenomenal year that followed, has made the achievement sweeter.

It was Martina who helped me relax on that fateful day of 12 April 2015. My journey would have been more difficult without someone like her beside me, someone who knew exactly what it was like to be on top of the world. She was a calming and soothing influence on me. Generally, she tends to be more animated than I am. But for this event our roles had been reversed. She was keeping it together for me as she knew I was dealing with a lot more than everyone else.

There was a flood of emotions and reactions with social media going berserk and the phones ringing non-stop. The exultation had begun back home in India, suitably at prime time. But away from it all, my father and I, accompanied by Martina and her agent, David Tosas, drove down for a quiet dinner in town. We barely spoke of what we had just achieved. We just felt enormously satisfied and relieved. We had pushed ourselves to the limits mentally and physically to even play in Charleston after an exhausting four weeks of tournaments in Indian Wells and Miami. The job was finally done and the goal achieved.

I flew back to Hyderabad the next day and had no time to celebrate. The Fed Cup had already begun and I joined the team as captain of India. Interestingly, I played my very first match as the World No. 1 doubles player back home in my city of Hyderabad, at the Lal Bahadur Shastri Stadium, where my journey had begun a decade earlier. This was the venue where I had won my first WTA singles title in 2005 to begin the march towards global success.

Everything I have achieved on the tennis courts in the last decade is only half the story. In this book I hope to recreate the other half as well. The story of years of struggle, of the methodical planning and single-minded dedication of 'Team Sania', the countless sacrifices – especially those made by my family – the pain and heartache, the shedding of sweat and blood, interspersed with priceless moments of exultation and glory. All this and more went into making me a multiple Grand Slam champion and the No. 1 player in the world.

1

THE FIRST MISS OF MY LIFE

OHIO, JANUARY 1991.

It was still early days for me and my family in the United States of America. We had migrated only a few months earlier. I was four years old. My father, just into his thirties, had taken the painfully risky decision to not just wind up his printing press back home in Hyderabad, but also to nip his nascent construction business in the bud.

It had been tough for him to achieve financial stability, ever since the death of my grandparents – my father was then barely out of his teens. Both his brother and sister were based in the US, which left him alone in India, fending for himself at a tender age. A decade later, after years of struggle, he was finally beginning to feel monetarily comfortable. It was then that my father's sister, my aunt Anjum, had called excitedly to break the news that our immigration papers were in the final stages of processing.

The green card that Dad had almost unwillingly applied for ten years earlier, after the demise of his parents, with a strong push from my aunt and uncle, had finally come through. Of course, his siblings had always wanted my father to move closer to them.

Dad, though, had long forgotten about the impending migration and it was more of an inconvenience to him now than anything else. He had since gotten married to my mother, Nasima, their first child

4

had been born, and he was carefully and diligently growing the modest printing business that he had established after starting off on a shoestring budget. For the first time, after a decade of struggle, things were finally falling into place.

It was after weeks of deliberation, of winding up affairs in Hyderabad and perhaps with mixed feelings that my father, mother and four-year-old me arrived in Springfield, Ohio to stay with Dad's brother, Kamran, and his family. My uncle was a brilliant engineer, who had moved to the United States nearly two decades earlier to further his career and to chase the 'American dream'.

'The migration to USA was one of the hardest decisions I've ever had to make. It meant uprooting the family at a time when we had just begun to establish ourselves,' my father would tell me years later. But within two months of landing in the US, he would make another choice that was to leave an indelible imprint on our minds.

*

Before beginning the serious task of earning a livelihood for themselves in USA, my parents decided to travel to California to visit Dad's sister, who lived there. We were booked on the US Air Flight 1493 from Columbus, Ohio to Los Angeles on 1 February 1991, a Friday.

A few days before our scheduled departure, my aunt called to suggest we change our flight bookings to Saturday, as it would be more convenient for her to pick us up from the airport on the weekend. My father made the change without realizing that it would turn out to be the most significant decision of our lives.

A day before our newly scheduled flight, my aunt called once more. I may not have noticed it then but in subsequent years, looking back again and again, I could relate to the look on my father's face as he heard what she had to say. It was an odd mix of relief and panic. By a strange twist of fate, the Friday flight that we were originally booked on had crashed into another aircraft while landing at Los Angeles airport, tragically killing twenty passengers and two members of the crew. By God's will, we had escaped. It was a miracle.

I was obviously too young to fully comprehend the magnitude of what had just transpired, the enormous blessing we had received. I was shielded from the gravity of the situation, as any young girl would be. Perhaps because I was the only child, my parents were careful to keep me away from any negativity, sometimes to a fault. I think this is something they are guilty of even today, although I now have a sibling.

At the time, it seemed like a lot of fuss over a 'missed' flight. But anytime one of us recalls that day, we shudder to think of what could have happened had my aunt not suggested that we change our flight booking.

My father switched on the news channels and watched in horror, and my mother nearly fainted when she saw the gruesome images. The next few hours were a whirlwind. Dad, Mom and my uncle's family debated at length whether we should risk boarding the same flight, 1493, on which we were booked exactly twenty-four hours later. Thankfully, good sense prevailed and my father settled the issue. 'If the same flight happens to crash on two consecutive days, we would have to consider ourselves a wee bit unlucky, don't you think?' he said, smiling.

My parents were on edge as we boarded a near empty flight on that Saturday morning. The atmosphere was rather gloomy. I was still protected by my young enthusiasm and childish innocence, but fear was written on every adult face around me. The handful of grown-ups who flew with us clearly endured a tense flight. My mother kept reciting prayers throughout the five-hour journey.

Finally it was over and we landed at the Los Angeles airport, to be greeted with bouquets and relief by my aunt, her family, and my father's cousins.

It was an unforgettable experience, but the most memorable part of it for me was what followed next. It was not just our family that had been waiting for us. A huge horde of television news crews had turned up too, to receive us. It was a dramatic story – 'The arrival of the brave passengers who flew fearlessly just twenty-four hours after the ill-fated flight 1493 had crashed the previous day'!

Our relieved faces were beamed out live on national television networks across USA. That was my first tryst with the media. I enjoyed the attention, bewildered but thrilled. I was asked to speak into the microphone on camera for a sound byte, but I could not. I was too shy then, having no clue whatsoever that dealing with the media would one day become a routine part of my life.

*

After spending some time at my aunt's home in San Diego, we came back to Springfield to live with my uncle.

My father set up a printing press all over again with leased equipment, forty-five miles away in Columbus. My mother took up a job in a nearby hospital as an assistant to a cardiologist, earning a minimum wage. The responsibility of taking care of me fell on my dad even as he went about meeting customers and organizing supplies.

With a little money coming into the family coffers, we moved into a cozy one-bedroom apartment in Columbus, not far from the print shop. It would be another year before I became eligible for public school. An expensive private education was out of the question, so there was no option but to wait till I was six years old.

From eight in the morning to seven in the evening, I would sit in the print shop, playing on a computer, talking to a few friendly customers, helping my father make some copies on the duplicating machines or just getting plain bored.

It was in Ohio around this time that I had my first brush with tennis.

Dad was playing doubles with three of his friends on the community courts on the weekend while my cousins, the twins Asif and Arif, and I picked balls for them. Finally, a couple of hours later, it was our turn to wave the rackets around and have some fun.

I was bursting with anticipation and could not wait to hit the stuffing off the tennis balls. I had picked up some cues and made a few mental notes while watching my dad and his friends play, but with the racket actually in hand, I had little success in making those shots that had looked so good in my imagination. Soon I was bullied off the court by my boisterous seven-year-old cousins, who never missed an opportunity to pull my leg.

But the experience was enough for me to want to play tennis. I was an athletic young girl who liked to spend more time outdoors than inside. I remember asking my mom to enrol me for tennis classes. She was heartbroken because she had to deny me this luxury they just could not afford. The classes would have cost around $40 an hour, way too much for them to set aside for a four-year-old when they were surviving hand-to-mouth, working long hours. My mother told me later that she cried when she was alone, overwhelmed at not being able to give her daughter what she so badly wanted.

Just like my education, tennis would have to wait.

My father hated watching me spend hours just sitting at the print shop when I should have been out playing with friends or in school. It was becoming difficult for him to escape the fact that they had come to the US for a better future for me, but here I was, sitting and whiling away my time for almost a year. In India, I had already attended classes in the primary section for over a year. But here, the lack of a steady education was a continuous reminder to him of the life we had left behind. Life in India had not been luxurious by any means, but had definitely offered more choices and possibilities.

My parents were earning just about enough to make ends meet, but the fact that my life was on hold with no clear plan and no assurances for the future in sight eventually made them decide that it was best to move back. This did not go down too well with our extended family, who thought we had lost our minds to be giving up on the land of everyone's dreams. But my dad knew exactly what he wanted for his family and he was unwilling to compromise. His own father had given up a life in England almost half a century ago to return to his motherland after completing his education and, in a way, history was repeating itself for this side of the Mirza family.

'That was the best decision I ever made in my life,' Dad told me many years later, when I was old enough to understand, and I think he was absolutely right.

In February 1992, our family moved back to India.

2

EARLY LESSONS

ONE OF THE first things my mother wanted to do when we returned to India was to enrol me for tennis classes. In the US, she had been forced by circumstances to deny her only child what she desired. The family could not afford it then. But she certainly could in India, and she was determined to give me what I had yearned for.

Once back in Hyderabad, she took me to the Nizam Club for my swimming lessons. The tennis courts were next to the pool and she met the coach to get me started. I was nearly six years old then.

I had rejoined Nasr School and was happy to be back in the company of my old classmates. Samia was my best friend and we would fight with the other kids to secure seats next to each other in class. She and her sisters were also to be enrolled for tennis classes. They were all much taller than I was. The coach looked at me, a tiny little girl, and refused pointblank to take me in, while Samia and her sisters were accepted. My mother fought tooth and nail with him, determined not to take no for an answer. 'What do you mean she's too young?' she argued with him. 'She's my daughter and I want her to learn tennis. If you don't teach her, I'll take her somewhere else.'

The coach was the affable Srikkanth, a twenty-two-year-old former national player who enjoyed coaching kids in his spare time. Faced with my mother's conviction, he had no option but to give me a chance. He asked me to hit a few balls with the others. I connected with my first stroke, while the others missed. Soon, I was striking the ball better than anyone else on the court and Srikkanth could not deny me a spot in his camp any more.

Thus it began. Together with swimming and roller-skating (my mother had enrolled me for these as well) tennis started to fill my hours. It did not take long for me to realize that I was quite talented at the racket game. Not just good, but far better than the others. I was a decent swimmer and roller-skater but tennis was different and I knew I had a flair for it. I was quickly making strides that would begin to separate me from the other kids in the camp. I just loved hitting the tennis ball and I would strive to clobber it as hard as I could. My timing was surprisingly good and every day I was getting better, enjoying it more and more. I was hooked.

A month into the lessons, I was already hitting proper forehands and backhands. Even my coach could hardly believe what he was witnessing. He had probably not seen a six-year-old middle the tennis ball so cleanly and with a power that belied her size. He would throw me balls that I smacked with great relish. I still remember that connect. Soon, it became more than just a sport I enjoyed. Improving myself became the fuel that propelled my engine. When you first realize you are really good at something, it begins to consume you. Within a few months tennis became the only focus of my life.

Thrilled with my progress, Srikkanth excitedly called my father one day, to urge him to watch me play. 'You have to come, sir! She has tremendous ball sense and timing. You cannot teach that. It's pure talent.'

My father had been a sports freak all his life and had spent his youth on the famous maidans of Mumbai, playing in the Kanga League alongside a number of notable cricketers. My grandfather had handpicked the best educational institutions for him to study at while also ensuring that cricket and sports were given due importance in the school's curriculum.

After the untimely death of my grandparents, Dad stopped playing cricket altogether. He even had to give up the post-graduation course in Cost Accountancy that he was pursuing. But though the struggle for survival suddenly became a necessity, sport remained his true love and passion. It was obviously a special treat for him to watch his daughter play tennis, a sport that he himself had indulged in occasionally. In some ways, my father started dreaming of a career in sports for me from the day he watched me play for the first time. A whisper of a thought at the back of his mind slowly became a loud voice in his head.

If my father was beside himself with joy on discovering my talent in a sport he so loved and enjoyed, he did not show it. He would have liked nothing more than to live his sporting dream vicariously, through me. He had never been a professional sportsman himself but his breeding was that of one. He came from a family of cricketers, and most of the men played the game at some level. There were club players, first-class and Test cricketers in his extended family and having been brought up in this environment, he was perfectly placed to nurture what he believed was a special talent in his own offspring.

My father understood that playing a sport professionally involved overcoming high intensity pressure even if one was possessed of talent, and he would always underplay the importance of winning so that I never came under undue pressure. All through my life, and especially while I was growing up, I was never made to feel as though tennis was my only option. I played because I enjoyed it, and my parents gave me to understand that I could continue to play for as long as I wanted to. But after that significant day, Dad started taking my tennis more seriously, keen as he was to see where this journey would take us.

My mother accompanied me to the courts every afternoon, after school, and my father started playing with me on the weekends. Thus began the Mirza family's love affair with the sport of tennis – a relationship that would endure and become the core around which our lives have now revolved for almost a quarter of a century.

Had it not been for a freak accident though, tennis may not have become a priority as early as it did.

I had begun to enjoy roller-skating as well and sometimes missed tennis to skate. My mother was even contemplating entering me for a State Ranking competition. Then one day, I fell on my head in the rink and fainted for a few seconds. The memory is still fresh after all these years – when I came back to my senses, my mother was on her knees beside me, crying and slapping me on the cheeks hysterically.

I did not get to see my roller-skates after that day. My mother was in a state of shock and paranoia for weeks. She never allowed me to skate again and did not tell my father about the incident until years later.

Giving up roller-skating shifted my focus entirely to tennis. My destiny was taking control.

*

We had settled down in the house that my father had built in Hyderabad. Dad's cousin Faiyaz and his family also lived with us, as they used to before we went away to the US. Faiyaz Chacha, who went on to play first-class cricket, was the anchor in Dad's life. When he lost his parents, Dad's own brother and sister were away in the US and it was Faiyaz Chacha who played the role of a brother to him. I called his mother, who was my grandfather's sister, 'Dadi ma'. His son Faraaz is a couple of years older than me and we were inseparable as kids.

My mother took over the small printing press that my parents had restarted in Hyderabad and Dad began to concentrate on the construction business that he had dabbled in before migrating to the US. Irrespective of how busy she was, I remained the focal point around which my mother's life revolved. And while it was my father with his knowledge of tennis who guided me throughout, it was my mother who played a pivotal role during those critical years by always being there to take care of everything else that was needed.

In the summer holidays, we went to Bengaluru to spend a few weeks with my father's uncle. It was Wimbledon time and my parents were watching Steffi Graf play Jana Novotna in the 1993 women's final on television. When I walked into the room, Dad looked at me indulgently and said to Mom, 'Hey, what if someday Sania becomes a professional tennis player and gets to play at Wimbledon on Centre Court?'

Everyone present in the room chuckled at the outrageous suggestion. In those days, it was quite unthinkable, the idea of playing tennis seriously and actually making a career of it, much less being a world-class women's player. But my mother, partly because she was naive about the game, took to the idea. She went teary-eyed and a smile brightened her face.

Mom knew exactly how important sport was to Dad. She understood very little about tennis then, but having watched the excitement of Wimbledon unfold on television, she knew what a major achievement it would be if her daughter actually made it to the famed Centre Court. 'If Sania has a chance of playing at Wimbledon, I won't leave a stone unturned to make it happen,' she said, rather prophetically.

As I was the only child in my family for the first seven years of my life, Mom and Dad devoted all their time to me. But financially, those were difficult days for my parents, something I realized later as an adult.

My mother with her printing press had more flexible working hours. Dad, on the other hand, was working eighteen hours a day, putting everything into his construction business while helping Mom with the press. So my mother ensured she worked around my tennis classes. In fact, I saw very little of my father in those years. By the time he came home from work, I would be fast asleep, exhausted after my tennis lessons. Although I wanted to stay up to see him, I could not keep my eyes open beyond eight at night. Sometimes, I would see him before being dropped off to school and then not till the next morning.

What I learnt from my father very early, even at that age, was that sport should be an essential part of one's routine. He truly believed that sport teaches us a lot about life. It was his conviction that a seven-year-old who has learned to deal with wins and losses would be better able, at thirty, to deal with anything that life might throw at her – certainly better than someone who has never played sports. Athletes handle losses on a daily basis. You have to dust yourself off after each painful loss and prepare for the next win, day after day. I grew up believing in this and am convinced that this attitude placed me ahead of most opponents I faced then and even much later in my career.

I quickly developed a passion for the game, but perhaps the biggest reason I pursued tennis seriously was because my family loved and believed in the sport. My parents put in so much effort without knowing if their sacrifices were going to lead anywhere. If they had started to count their losses and the extremely hard-earned money – which, to the uninvolved bystander, seemed to be going down the drain – they would perhaps have never given my tennis career the kind of support they did. They would have pulled the plug even before we could discover if I stood a chance on the world stage.

*

In temperament, I have always been a lot like my mother. We are both fairly impulsive. But that also means we are doers. If my mother wants to do something, she does not wait till the next day. She goes out and does it right away. The impatient streak in me often makes me impulsive. But at the same time, I am a very easy-going person. My mother, from her fashion sense to the sacrifices she has made for me over the years, has been a huge influence in my life.

A year into my tennis lessons, my mother was pregnant with my sister, Anam, and it was not feasible for her to endure the bumpy rides in rickety autos any more. We got special permission to play in an exclusive club nearby where Srikkanth would train me. Even though she was near full-term with my sister, my mother would accompany me to the court, walking about a kilometre every day.

My father's enthusiasm and uncanny knack for the sport, my mother's diligence, their sacrifices together, our experience of living in the US, the sporting culture and background of our family, the

3

GETTING A GRIP

Tennis in Hyderabad was still developing in those days and no one in India would have honestly believed that the country could produce a Grand Slam women's player in the foreseeable future. But my father had a very keen eye. He was a club-level tennis player who was perhaps more proficient in cricket than in the game of rackets, but he had followed the sport for decades with a clinical mind and a passion that defied logic. In fact, soon after he graduated from Mumbai University, he had even published and edited a local sports magazine in Hyderabad which covered and offered critical analysis of tennis among other sports.

It could be these vital experiences from my father's early life that prepared him for what then seemed a virtually impossible task, of producing a world-class women's tennis player from India. It was a mission that he undertook passionately, with meticulous attention to detail and remarkable foresight in the years that followed. He may not have had the opportunity to be a sportsman himself but surprisingly, he possessed the knowledge, temperament and ability to nurture a professional tennis player. Every coach who worked with me added to my game in his own way, but it was my father who helped maintain the continuity and equilibrium in my learning process while working overtime to keep himself abreast of the changing trends and techniques in the tennis world.

'Sania can become the state champion one day if she works hard,' a coach told my parents in those early days. It was around this time that my forehand, a crucial part of my game, began to take its current shape. My forehand is easily my biggest weapon and was primarily responsible for catapulting me to a career-high singles ranking of No. 27 and doubles ranking of No. 1 in the world, apart from helping me win three Grand Slam titles in women's doubles and three in mixed doubles. But it did not always look like it does today.

I was seven years old and loved smacking the ball with all the power that I could muster. I also had a very special gift of timing. However, I had an extreme western forehand grip, which made it difficult for me to lift the lower trajectory balls. My coach happened to come across an article in a tennis magazine in which an identical case, of a seven-year-old girl with a pronounced western forehand grip like mine, was discussed. In that piece, a world renowned coach described at length the strategy he had adopted to ensure that the highly talented girl realized her potential to the fullest.

He explained that there was no chance a seven-year-old girl would develop a wrist strong enough to be able to lift the low balls, given the awkward way in which she held the racket. If it had been a boy in a similar situation, he might have let him continue with his unique grip and concentrate on developing strength in the wrist and forearm muscles for support. Since this particular girl had tremendous timing, he was careful not to upset that rhythm and started working on changing her grip gradually, over a period of six months, until it stabilized.

My coach and Dad decided to work on the same lines with my forehand technique and over the next few months, I gradually shifted my grip until I reached a point that was 70 per cent closer to where I needed to be according to the coaching manual. Then suddenly, no matter what my coach or father said, I refused to change it any more. I knew even as a seven-year-old that I had found the forehand grip that suited me and I was confident enough to live with it. My coach gave up and I stuck to the semi-western grip that I use even today.

It was many years later that a group of technical experts analyzed my game when I tasted some success at Wimbledon. They concluded that it was my grip along with the unique flick of my wrist that gave me the phenomenal power on my forehand.

Their analysis led them to a few more interesting observations and conclusions. My grip could be taught to any young player, they felt, and the movement of the wrist, though unique, could be imbibed by a few who were loose-jointed. But in order to use these together to generate the kind of power and precision that I was capable of, the person would need to be endowed with a tremendous ball sense and very special timing. This, in the experts' collective opinion, was not something that could be taught; one had to be born with it. I have to consider myself very fortunate to have been gifted with these rare abilities and this is one more reason for me to believe that someone up there wanted me to succeed in tennis.

I believe the forehand alone could not have guaranteed my success if I was not bred to be aggressive on the court. Here, again, my father was a key influence. As a club cricketer, he once told me, he had been defensive in his approach, unable to play the kind of offensive shots that he admired in his cricketing idols. That always rankled him, I think. So whether I won or lost, it was absolutely crucial for him that I played aggressively and he always encouraged me to be flamboyant in my stroke play. As long as I had tried my best, a loss was not to be rued. It was something one could use to improve one's game. That is how I learned to go for broke, a trait that became my trademark in years to come. I did not always win with this temperament, but I was never a boring player to watch.

Secondly, my father firmly believed that at the very top, you do not win by just waiting for others to commit mistakes. He inculcated the 'take the bull by the horns' approach in me. 'Controlled aggression and the ability to produce winners under pressure are the only traits that separate a winner from the rest on the biggest stage,' he would tell me.

There are those who feel that my forehand makes it easy for me to beat my opponents, but I know that the full benefit of it came about only because I was trained to be fearless.

4

THE FIRST BREAKTHROUGH

MY YOUNGER SISTER, Anam, was born in February 1994 and I was very excited. I could not keep my eyes off the adorable little girl and I rushed home from school every afternoon to play with her. The only problem was that I now had to share my mom with her and that could sometimes get annoying. My father began to escort me to the tennis courts instead of my mother, who needed to spend more time with my little sister. Apart from that, not much changed after Anam's arrival as school and tennis kept me well occupied.

Despite my tennis gaining more momentum and significance, my interest in school never lessened. I had always been a bright and conscientious student who hated missing classes for any reason whatsoever. I was the kid with the 100 per cent attendance record at school, something I held dear and would not allow to be broken at any cost. I certainly refused to miss school for tennis.

In fact, as a young girl, I dreamt of becoming a doctor, to follow in the footsteps of one of my cousins who had recently got admission into medical school. What helped me keep up with both, my tennis lessons and my school work, was that I had a very sharp memory and the capacity to absorb information very quickly. There were many days when I was unable to finish my homework after coming back from tennis lessons and crashing early. My mother would then read out the chapters or long poems in the car while my father drove us to school in the morning and I would memorize it all before we reached. That's how I prepared for many of my examinations.

*

I was eight years old when I played my maiden State Ranking Junior Tournament in Hyderabad and lost in the second round, trying to be over-aggressive without much success. However, I cherished the award I received for being the most talented junior in the tournament.

The first time the tennis fraternity of Hyderabad and the local sports correspondents took notice of me was when I beat a 5' 10" giant of a girl, who was almost twice my age, in an Under-16 State Ranking tournament. The girl had played in the national tournaments and was considered a powerful stroke maker. I was short in stature for my age and barely topped the net. This perhaps made my opponent feel I was too small for her.

Seeing that I could not put a ball back in the warm-up, she moved forward towards the net and smilingly asked me to play from the service box. I was thoroughly embarrassed and overawed by the occasion as almost a hundred members of the club had gathered to watch the game.

But when the match began, I started to feel more comfortable and rediscovered my ability to strike the ball sweetly. In less than thirty minutes, the crowd had been stunned into disbelief as I struck the ball with power and accuracy to the corners of the court and worked up a 6-1 lead in the best-of-fifteen match. After my opponent hit back to even the score at 6-all, I held my nerve to carve out an 8-6 win. I still remember the sight of my opponent walking to the side of the court and bawling her eyes out.

That was the first time I started to believe that I was really good. I was just eight, still very young, but I knew I was on to something special. My parents too began to take my game more seriously. The win earned me thunderous applause and big headlines in the local media the next day.

'Tiny Sania hogs limelight' said the headline in the *Indian Express* – one of many clippings that found a place in the scrapbook I used to maintain in my junior days.

I started practising more and more. From one hour it became two and three, and then five hours a day, until I had no time for anything else. For many years, it was just school in the morning and tennis and swimming after that. Going to family weddings was the only break I got from my routine, when I would allow myself a well-earned holiday of three or four days to enjoy the joyful cacophony of my relatives. My mother was one of ten brothers and sisters. So I had many weddings to attend as a young child and even more cousins to make each one an occasion to remember.

That summer, I won my first tennis title and surprisingly, it came in the Under-16 mixed doubles event at the Gymkhana Courts in Secunderabad. Fittingly, I received the trophy for my maiden title from Ghulam Ghouse, the former deputy governor of the Reserve Bank of India and an old, dear friend of my late grandfather.

A die-hard tennis fanatic, Mr Ghouse had four sons, who had all turned out to be prominent national and state ranked tennis players. His grandson Mustafa kept up the family tradition and became a national champion in later years. My father had grown up virtually at the feet of Ghulam Ghouse, when the two sports loving families were based in Mumbai, and it could well be that some part of his inspiration, his keen encouragement of me, derived from the grand old man himself.

The inspiration to mould my tennis career could have also come in some measure from Ghulam Ahmed, India's former cricket captain, who was the husband of my father's maternal cousin, besides being a childhood mate of my grandfather. After the death of my grandparents, Dad had grown extremely close to the world renowned off-spinner and he always remained a big influence on my father as a mentor.

Soon after I turned nine, I became the Hyderabad Schools Tennis Champion in my age group and it was decided that I would now travel to Bengaluru to compete in my first tournament away from home. It was Christmas time and I played in the Under-10 Karnataka State Ranking tournament at Mahila Seva Samaj. I won the early rounds with aplomb and by the time I reached the final on the eve of the New Year, I was aware of the presence of a decent fan following, an audience that enjoyed watching my go-for-broke style of tennis.

My biggest fan was probably Dad's cousin, Rishad Taher, whom I called 'Babu Chacha'. He has lived all his life in Bengaluru, has a wonderful sense of humour, and has stood by Dad through thick and thin since the time they were kids. Over the years, he has become equally close to me, Anam and my mom and is very much a part of our immediate family. He was fascinated by my aggressive tennis when he watched me play that day in Bengaluru and has been my die-hard supporter ever since.

In the final of that tournament, I lost to the local girl, Maithri Jagannath, who kept lobbing the ball back and pushed me into making errors after a few aggressive strokes. When I received the runners-up trophy, one of the spectators came on to the court to present me with a small gift and then asked for an autograph. It was the first time in my life that anyone had asked me for one and I was thrilled. The lady then said to me, 'One day you will win Wimbledon, my child, and I will treasure your autograph.'

*

I played in a number of State Ranking tournaments the following year and began to dominate the Under-14 section in my home state of Andhra Pradesh, winning a handful of trophies. I also travelled to Mumbai in my summer holidays and won the Under-12 Maharashtra State Ranking title for good measure.

These matches prepared me well for the All India Tennis Association (AITA) circuit and I had some impressive wins in the South Zone tournaments that were held in November that year. Since I was a keen student, I refused to skip school to travel for matches. I was clear I did not want my studies to suffer and was willing to give up tennis but not school. Thankfully, my mother connived to use the influence of my headmistress, Mrs Ali Khan, to convince me to go. Hailing from an illustrious family of sportsmen, Mrs Khan was the sister of former Indian cricket captain, Late Mansur Ali Khan, the Nawab of Pataudi.

'In order to achieve something in life, one has to sacrifice a few things, Sania,' she explained gently after summoning me to her office. 'You can catch up on your lessons after you come back from the tournaments and still do well in your exams. You have a special talent for tennis and you must pursue the game.'

Travel was a huge financial drain on our family. My parents worked tirelessly to save every rupee they could. My mother would request letters from the Andhra Pradesh Lawn Tennis Association (APLTA) to avail of special discounts that athletes were entitled to, on second-class train tickets for tournament travel. She would then go to the railways office to get an official stamp of approval. Finally, she would stand in queues for hours at the station to book tickets, often returning empty-handed because the station master had refused the discount as he had never heard of the scheme. But an 80 per cent discount on train tickets was hard to resist. It even allowed us the flexibility of tentative bookings, since the exact date of travel depended on my match results.

It was around this time that we started travelling by car for most tournaments. It was the most convenient and affordable form of transport, considering that our travel dates depended on how deep I went into the draw. Flights were too expensive and train bookings weren't always available at short notice.

My father would drive us in the old Maruti 1000 that he had 'dieselized' – a huge investment at the time, made specifically for my tennis travel. We logged thousands of miles in that vehicle over the next three years. The foursome of Mom, Dad, little Anam and I drove several times to Vijayawada, Eluru, Bengaluru, Chennai, Pondicherry, Thiruvananthapuram, Madurai, Coimbatore, Mumbai, Pune, Nagpur and Ahmedabad for various tournaments. I spent far more time in the car than on the courts.

We would try to keep the expenses to a minimum by staying in extremely modest budget hotels. Every rupee saved could be spent on another tournament to get me more exposure.

I remember us driving into Ahmedabad for one such tournament. It was already past midnight as we entered the city after a brief halt in Mumbai. But, as usual, arriving in a city was the start of another journey altogether – the search for a cheap, affordable place to stay in. After driving around for more than an hour, we found ourselves a 7 ft x 6 ft room with a single bed that was barely large enough for the four of us to even sit on it comfortably. I slept with my head on my mother's lap while my father and Anam curled up on the floor.

Once, in Chennai, we stayed in a remote lodge which was not connected by a proper road or even a 'kutcha' lane. We had to park our car half a kilometre away as that was the closest a vehicle could get to that dingy little place. It was in the middle of nowhere but the price was right.

Travel in the Maruti 1000 was tiresome, especially the thirty-hour drives from Hyderabad to Thiruvananthapuram or Ahmedabad. But by no means was it boring.

The time spent on the road was not only crucial in preparing me for the long, difficult path ahead as a tennis player, but also gave me some of the fondest memories of us together as a family. It bonded the four of us in ways no expensive vacation in the world's best hotels could have. I always look back on those endless days and nights, the highways and the small dusty streets, the tiny, dimly lit rooms in lacklustre hotels, the early morning starts and late night arrivals, the faces of the people on the road, the smiles we encountered at our various pit stops, the applause of the scanty crowds at tournaments, the tiny plastic trophies won and many more lost, as a time of innocence – when our lives were still linked closely enough to afford us countless hours together as a family.

5

AN UNFORGETTABLE EXPERIENCE

THE ROAD WAS a fun place, by and large, but once in a while things could get scary and messy, especially for a young child. All I wanted was to play tennis, win matches and inch closer to my dream, but sometimes it became virtually a matter of life and death.

It was 1999 – a year that was critical for my development as one of the best juniors of the country. AITA had announced that the top three ranked players in the Under-14 category would represent India in the World Junior Championships in Jakarta in May that year and I was prepared to give an arm and a leg to play for my country.

I performed consistently to come within striking distance of a place in the junior national team but I still needed to make it at least to the semi-final in a tournament in Guwahati to clinch my spot. That trip proved to be one of the most horrifying experiences of my life.

My father and I left by train for Kolkata on a Thursday evening. It was to be a twenty-four-hour journey. After spending a day in the city, we were to board a flight to Guwahati on Sunday morning to be in time for the tournament that was to kick off on Monday. But our train ran twelve hours late due to a problem on the tracks and instead of reaching Kolkata at seven in the evening on Friday, it arrived at Kharagpur railway station at six on Saturday morning. We must have been about 100 miles from Kolkata when we were informed that the train would go no further: a bandh had been declared across West Bengal.

After several hours, a local train drew up on the adjacent platform and we were asked to board it. They would try to run that train through to Kolkata, we were told. It was a chaotic scene as thousands of passengers abandoned our train in a hurry, attempting to get on to the local, armed with their baggage and with a determination to find the best spot. Some even climbed up on to the roof. We watched the drama unfold while holding on to the edge of our seats in the train we had been asked to de-board. After a bit of contemplation, my father decided we would stay put.

The scrambled exodus continued unabated and we wondered if we would be the only two people left behind. Another girl from Hyderabad, Manjusha, who was also travelling for the tournament with her parents, had met us during the journey. Fortunately, they too decided to stay behind with us in the abandoned train in which, eventually, not more than a dozen passengers remained.

We sat there anxiously, just staring at each other's faces as we prayed and hoped for information that would tell us we had made the right choice. Half an hour later, news filtered in that the other train, carrying thousands of passengers, had been stopped by a group of agitators ten miles away. The travellers were stranded in the middle of nowhere.

We seemed to have made the right choice by staying on in the near-empty train but had no idea what to do next. There were hardly any people at the station but groups of about twenty agitating men would march by every hour, shouting slogans and waving flags. Dusk was fast approaching and the growing darkness outside seemed eerie. It had been almost forty-eight hours since we left Hyderabad.

News trickled in that the bandh had got extended to the next day and that's when my father decided it was time for some drastic measures. Dad and Manjusha's father left us in the charge of her mom in the deserted compartment and decided to go out looking for another means of transport to Kolkata. They were gone for more than an hour but they came back with a plan.

My father had spoken to a private taxi driver, who had agreed to drive us to Kolkata when the sun went down, though at an exorbitant price. The driver first took Dad to the house of a local politician, who seemed to have some clout. He requested him for a letter addressed to the supporters of the cause, asking them to allow our group of five to travel in a taxi, despite the bandh, on medical grounds.

Dad returned with the letter in his hand and the driver by his side. Around 8 p.m. we carried our bags out of the desolate railway station but as my father was loading our luggage into the boot of the taxi, the lid slipped and came down heavily on his head. Blood gushed out almost in a torrent and trickled down onto his clothes. One look at him and I felt sick in the stomach and vomited all around me.

The wound was nasty and in the pitch darkness that enveloped us, we desperately tried to find a doctor to treat him. Blood continued to ooze from his forehead and it was clear he would need an anti-tetanus injection. There was hardly anyone on the streets but thankfully, the driver and his assistant were familiar with the area. They finally found a doctor's house and their loud knocking on the door added to the tension in the air. They requested the doctor to treat my father, which he did, and we finally got onto the highway at about 10.30 p.m.

With Dad sandwiched between the driver and his assistant on the front seat and me at the back with Manjusha's family, our vehicle of survival moved ahead. Every few miles, a noisy group of people would stop the car with sticks and lamps in their hands. The driver and his assistant would hop off and show them the letter from the politician and after some discussion and occasionally a heated argument in the local dialect, we would be allowed to move on.

We then reached a spot where there were about fifty people armed with burning bamboo sticks in their hands, looking menacing. The driver stoically informed us that they were from the rival party and would not heed the politician's letter that we had. No amount of cajoling would work. It was time to buckle up. So we locked our car from inside and sped past the screaming crowd, with several of the men trying to stop us in our tracks.

Barely a hundred yards away, another group of agitated men ran towards our cab with sticks in their hands. They shouted slogans and it seemed as though they were preparing to attack the group that we had just breezed past. We found ourselves in the midst of a gang war, precariously positioned on the highway on the night of a bandh, hundreds of miles away from home.

The driver moved swiftly. He swerved the taxi off the road and drove through the fields, zipping past the group that we had earlier avoided. They tried to attack us but we managed to get through. We drove back some way and took refuge in a roadside eatery.

'We've had enough! Please drop us off at any nearby hotel. There are children with us,' my father said to the driver.

'There's no hotel in the vicinity, sir,' the driver replied. He wrote out the address of his home on a scrap of paper. 'The local people will never harm an outsider, so you are safe. But if I should get killed, please send my vehicle to this address,' he said. We were stunned into silence.

On his advice, we waited for over an hour at the dhaba until, in the driver's opinion, the gang war had come to an end. He then drove us to the city of Kolkata and no further incidents troubled us on the way. It was past midnight by the time we found a small hotel near the airport to check into.

We caught the early morning flight to Guwahati, just in time to sign in for the tournament. Soon after we reached our hotel, we heard the news that a bomb had exploded at a spot that we had crossed twenty minutes earlier, on the way from the airport to the tennis club. Apparently, there had been an unsuccessful attempt to assassinate a prominent politician.

I was so shaken by our journey that at that point, the outcome of the tournament seemed the least of my concerns. But I actually felt relieved when I finally got on to the court to compete. I tried to forget the ordeal we had just undergone and played well to reach the semi-final.

Five days later, through with the tournament, we reached the airport in the morning to board a flight to Kolkata, from where we were booked on the train back to Hyderabad. Once again, we were caught in a maddening chaos. A bomb scare had created panic and caused all flights to be indefinitely delayed. We hung around restlessly at the airport for almost twelve hours until our aircraft was cleared for take-off at 10 p.m.

In Kolkata, we took a taxi to the Howrah railway station and hunted for a lodge nearby to spend the six hours before the departure of our train. We found a rickety old place around midnight where falling asleep, regardless of how tired we were, was not an option. We tossed and turned for a few hours, trying to get some rest, and then wheeled our bags out at four in the morning for the walk to the station, which was more than a kilometre away.

We got into the compartment at the break of dawn to begin the last leg of a journey that had already proved to be dangerously eventful. Tired beyond expression and emotionally drained, we dragged ourselves to our seats. We just did not have the strength to go through one more stressful ordeal. We needed to rest and sleep.

I lay down on the sleeper berth and my eyes fell on an article in the morning newspaper that was in Dad's hand. The Junior National team had been announced. I went through the piece anxiously and stopped as I saw my name. I screamed in joy, relief flooding every inch of my body. Even as the other passengers stared at me curiously, I shouted, 'I am in! I am playing for India!'

I had clinched the coveted spot in the Under-14 Indian team. It would be my first chance ever to wear the national colours.

6

JUNIOR 'HIGH'

AT TWELVE YEARS of age, I was the baby of the Junior National team that included my state mate, Sasha Abraham, and Mumbai's Isha Lakhani. Mayur Vasanth was our coach on the tour. We performed well as a team in Jakarta and I flew back to begin what proved to be an amazing run on the Indian junior circuit.

AITA had started a new format with the aim of reducing the travel undertaken by the juniors. A player could opt to compete in any one of the four zones that the circuit had been divided into. The string of tournaments would be held twice a year and the best four players from each zone would compete in the Masters at New Delhi in an elite draw of sixteen.

North was the toughest zone, followed by West, South and then East. I had done fairly well in the South Zone circuit in my first stint on the national scene. I decided to test myself in the West the following season and after notching up some decent results, went on to play in North Zone. It was here, in June-July 1999, soon after my return from Jakarta, that I really started making waves on the national stage.

I completely dominated the circuit, winning six out of the eight Under-14 and Under-16 titles in North Zone. This earned me a place in the Adidas Masters in New Delhi, where I competed against the best juniors in the country – the four top players from each zone. The field boasted the cream of Indian tennis, including Nandita Chandrashekhar, Megha Vakaria, Samrita Sekhar, Lata Asudhani,

Priyanka Parekh and the Bhambri sisters amongst others. I went on to win an impressive double – not just the Under-14 but also the Under-16 crown. I was only twelve years old.

It was a performance that stunned both, the tennis fans and the sports media in the country. Perhaps this was the first time in the history of Indian tennis that a female player had begun to achieve this degree of success even before entering her teens.

Victories tend to be inspiring, and perhaps it was after my twin wins in the Adidas Masters that I realized that playing tennis professionally was what I wanted to do most in my life. The mental shift was crystal clear to me. A career in tennis was what I would pursue even though I knew at the back of my mind that in this highly competitive field, in which no Indian woman had ever succeeded, I would need to be lucky to be successful, even with all my talent and willingness to work hard.

With the complete domination of the junior circuit, I had proved to myself that I possessed the ability to achieve greater laurels on a bigger stage. I now started to believe that becoming a successful professional tennis player, although difficult, was a distinct possibility. My emphatic performance in the Masters helped me get my first sponsorship deal from Adidas and the partnership has endured till today.

Deciding to pursue a career in sport is a big commitment, both emotionally and financially, and the risks are high. When one pays money to enrol in medical school, there is some assurance that five years down the line one will emerge as a full-fledged doctor. There were no such guarantees in the profession that had caught my fancy.

As the days went by, I worked with different coaches in Hyderabad, for various reasons. My first coach was Srikkanth. I moved to Ravi Chander, then Ganesh Raman, and finally settled with Prahalad Jain. Later, after I turned professional, I often hit with 'Chubby' Narendranath whenever I came home from the tour. He even travelled with me on the 2006 US Open circuit. None of the Indian coaches had the experience of producing a top-level international tennis player. What they did have was sincerity, which was apparent in the way they devoted their time to help fine-tune my game to the best of their abilities.

In August 1999, I became the No. 1 ranked player in India in the Under-14 category and started to concentrate more on the Under-16 events. I topped that group in the country in June 2000 and from then on, focused my efforts towards achieving success at the international level in the 18 & Under ITF (International Tennis Federation) tournaments.

On my thirteenth birthday, I debuted in my first international 18 & Under ITF World Ranking tournament in Islamabad and made an immediate impact that week, reaching the final in singles and winning the doubles title with Pakistan's star player, Nida Waseem, as my partner. The competition was mediocre and short of world-class but it helped me get a foot into the international arena.

I continued to dominate the AITA tournaments, scoring emphatic wins all over the country, though my focus was now the international circuit. Two AITA tournaments still linger in my memory. The first was a final that I played in Hyderabad against a player who was being touted as one of my biggest rivals.

I remember being down a match point when I heard a popular song from a Govinda film that was being played in a nearby marriage hall. Subconsciously, I started to sing to myself and did a little jig (a la Govinda) on the baseline, while receiving the serve. When I realized what I was doing, I smiled to myself. Not only did I hit a winner on that particular return, but I also went on to turn the tables and win the match against the stunned Junior No. 3, whom I had already beaten more than half a dozen times in that season.

Some of the media men had watched me do the little dance when I was a match point down and after I had won, they asked me about it. When I answered honestly, it made quite a story in the local press!

The other tournament that comes to mind is the Under-16 event that I played in Mumbai in April 2000. I did not lose a single game as I went about annihilating all my opponents with a score-line of

6-0, 6-0 until I reached the final, where I beat Isha Lakhani 6-2, 6-3 to capture the title.

During this period, I lost an occasional match and that would become big news on the sports pages. But the wins in the AITA tournaments gave me very little satisfaction in the absence of challenging opponents and I did not feel the thrill any longer. There were times when I got bored in these one-sided matches and would lose concentration to go down a couple of breaks. Then I would re-focus and come back to win. I knew, at the back of my mind, that when I needed to step on the gas, I would do it.

Looking back, I wonder if perhaps it was this tactic from my junior days, when lack of top-level competition allowed me the liberty to switch on and off, that was responsible for my concentration lapses in later years even when facing world-class opponents. I would inexplicably lose focus, relax, and then make a special effort to claw my way back. It took me many years on the professional circuit to overcome, or at least minimize, this particular weakness.

On the international junior circuit, my performance had become quite consistent and I soon broke into the top-250 players of the world. I travelled extensively to several countries to play in World Ranking tournaments and the financial strain on the family was increasing with every outing. I needed a sponsor to take care of the growing tour expenses.

G.V. Krishna Reddy of the GVK Group came forward to sponsor me in June 2000. At a time when no one believed that it was possible for an Indian woman to make a name for herself in international tennis, Mr Reddy, an avid club-level player himself, showed remarkable foresight and understanding of the game in agreeing to sponsor me. Initially, the support was for a modest amount but Mr Reddy's terms were clear – perform, and the sponsorship would continue and grow. For more than a decade, I wore the GVK logo on my sleeve with a great sense of pride.

My performances on the Asian ITF circuit were encouraging and by December, I was already ranked No.1 in India in the Under-18 category. I now wanted to test myself in the US, where I'd been told the game was played at a much higher level.

With the ranking that I had achieved by playing on the Asian circuit, I found myself seeded quite high in the tournaments that I entered in the US, but I was brought down to earth rather rudely when I failed to win even one singles match in four weeks of competition. I did have a semi-final showing in doubles at Dallas to give me some kind of encouragement and respite but the fierce competition that I faced in the US shook me.

At the end of the tour, I remember my father asking me if I felt I would ever be able to raise my game to the level that I had seen in the US. 'Not yet, but I know I can match them in six months' time,' I said, thoughtfully.

I had got a glimpse of what I needed to do to move up and the challenge of matching the best junior players of the world egged me on. I targeted playing at Wimbledon in 2001 but a lot of work was required to be done in order to qualify. I would have to break into the top forty-six in the world to be assured of an entry into the main draw and in order to do that, I needed to win a lot more matches.

I set about the task of improving my ranking in real earnest and with single-minded dedication. Titles came my way with some regularity and by June 2001, I had improved my ranking to fifty. I was now tantalizingly close to getting a chance to play at Wimbledon – just one place out of the main draw. Then one of the higher ranked seeds decided to withdraw from the juniors' draw in order to concentrate on her professional career and I moved in to become the youngest player to compete in any event at Wimbledon that year, at the age of fourteen years and seven months.

*

June 2001. I felt on top of the world as I entered Wimbledon Park for a practice session. It was wonderful to be rubbing shoulders with the likes of the Williams sisters, Lindsay Davenport and Jennifer Capriati among other superstars at the Aorangi Park Practice Pavilion.

However, I was still a relatively unknown player and most coaches thought it would be a waste of time for their players to hit with an upstart from a country that did not have much of a history in women's tennis. So I practised with Dad and hoped that someday I would come back as a good enough player to showcase my skills on the Centre Court at Wimbledon.

I played the British wild card, Julia Smith, in the first round, feeling nervous and jittery when the match began. Court no. 15 was packed with Indian faces and they were a source of great inspiration for me as I soon overcame my nerves and began to strike the ball with a lot more confidence and authority after having lost the first set.

The frenzy that broke out when I finally won the closely contested three-set match is one of my sweetest memories of Wimbledon. I was mobbed by my countrymen and signed more autographs that day than I had ever done. It was my maiden victory in the most famous tennis arena in the world and the thrill that I experienced was something special, even if I was destined to go down 6-1, 6-2 in the second round to Gisela Dulko.

That night, we went out for dinner to an Indian restaurant to celebrate and I was suddenly being recognized on the streets of London. I had an off the next day and it was way past midnight when I finally fell asleep, exhausted but fulfilled.

7

THE AFRICAN SAFARI

I WAS STRUGGLING for results in the Junior ITF season in the summer of 2002 and wins were hard to come by. The pressure from the sponsors to perform was constantly increasing with every loss and I was conscious of this. I also needed to do well enough to qualify for the US Open Juniors that was coming up in September.

We planned a four-week tour of the African continent in July-August. This included a couple of tournaments in Johannesburg, followed by one in Cairo, and the circuit would wind down in Gaborone, Botswana. I won both the doubles titles in Johannesburg and a singles crown in the second tournament, where I beat another Indian, Isha Lakhani, in the final. With this improved showing, I was in a much better frame of mind as I took the flight from Cairo to Gaborone, not knowing what lay in store for us in the country famed for its wild animals.

My father had been in touch with one of the organizers in Gaborone and had been advised that our visas would be stamped on arrival. Somebody would meet us at the airport with the required papers to enable us to enter the country. 'That is the general procedure in Botswana,' the official said.

We were a bit concerned when we didn't find anybody from the tennis fraternity in the arrival area. We were made to sit in the immigration room and wait. An hour later, it dawned on us that no one seemed to be on the way.

My father found a public telephone booth and called the organizer's number, only to discover that the line had been cut. We asked around a bit anxiously and were surprised to discover that several numbers in the city had been changed overnight. We got the new number almost two hours after landing in Gaborone and thankfully got through to the organizer.

'Oh, you've come? Great! We'll see you there in five minutes,' he said. We had to wait for two more hours before the gentleman actually made his way into the immigration room at the airport. 'I'm Bill,' he said, and after exchanging pleasantries, my father said, 'Where are the papers you were supposed to bring for us to get our visas?'

'I don't have any papers,' he said, matter-of-factly. 'The concerned person is not available today as he is busy and I am just filling in for him. I'll have to go back to the city to try and do something to help you clear immigration.' He was gone for another couple of hours while we waited patiently. With no more flights expected, the officers had decided they were done for the day and preferred to catch up on their sleep on the benches that were placed next to their tables. If there had been a flight out of Gaborone in the next few hours, we would have been on it even if it cost us a whopping amount!

But Bill finally returned – this time with a letter from an army officer, requesting the immigration official to grant us entry into the country of Botswana. The tactic seemed to work and sometime after midnight, we trooped out of the airport with the paperwork finally complete.

Once outside, we were taken aback when Bill asked us to get into a three-wheeler 'auto' – the kind that are used in India to carry groceries to the wholesale market or to transport lambs to the slaughter house. We hung on for dear life for the next hour as the vehicle swerved along the bumpy roads leading to the city. It was 2 a.m. when we finally checked into the hotel, which thankfully was quite comfortable.

The tournament went smoothly for me in sharp contrast to the problems we had negotiated to get into the city of Gaborone. I won the singles as well as the doubles titles with a fair degree of comfort despite eating very little. My appetite had dwindled thanks to the menu that was on offer during the course of the tournament. I have always considered myself to be a thoroughbred non-vegetarian but fox meat and snake delicacies were a bit too much for my taste.

A big prize distribution and cultural programme had been organized at the end of the final game but we had a flight to catch. Since it was nearing departure time, I requested the organizers to wrap up the function as soon as possible or else exempt us from the rest of the ceremonies as the next flight was available only after three days.

'You cannot miss this great programme we've organized. You don't have to worry, the flights never leave on time in Gaborone,' Bill explained, with a calm that failed to soothe Dad's ruffled nerves.

After the completion of an impressive ceremony, we finally reached the airport at 5.45 p.m., this time in a car, for a scheduled departure of 6 p.m. Sure enough, the flight was delayed. But at least we were not going to be stuck in Gaborone for the next three days! A successful, not to mention eventful, tour of the African continent thus came to an end. I had managed to win back the confidence of my sponsors with my performances during this tour and cemented my place in the main draw of the US Open Juniors. My future in tennis looked bright once again.

8

PLAYING FOR INDIA

I won my first professional women's ITF title in my home city of Hyderabad in September. I made full use of the wild card in the $10,000 ITF women's tournament which was sponsored by the GVK Group, to win the title and then went on to add a handful of singles and doubles trophies to my collection.

However, I can never forget the thrill of being selected to represent India in the Asian Games for the first time in 2002. The Games were to be held in October that year in Busan, South Korea. The feeling of walking out for your national flag for the first time stays with you forever.

Nirupama Vaidyanathan, the torch-bearer of women's tennis in India, was making a comeback to the game after her marriage. I was already being regarded as the up-and-coming player who would go on to take her place. But because Nirupama had taken a break, my ranking was better than hers and this meant that I was to play the No. 1 players from the countries we were drawn to play against. When we stepped out onto the court that October, I was about a month short of my sixteenth birthday.

We were a large contingent. For the first time in my career, I was in the company of the 'biggies' of Indian tennis – the best in the men's and women's categories. It was something special, rubbing shoulders with the finest in the country at an event like the Asian Games – my first big multi-nation, multi-discipline contest away from home.

Moreover, I was to play the mixed doubles with none other than Leander Paes, who was India's top-ranked player.

By June of that year, Mahesh Bhupathi, one of India's foremost doubles players, had already decided to play with Manisha Malhotra. Leander Paes, the other half of the great 'Indian Express' combine of those days, did not have a partner. He had walked up to Dad one day, a few months before the Asiad, and asked if I would partner him in the mixed doubles.

It was a great honour for me. I was hugely excited just to share the court with the accomplished doubles specialist that Leander was. For a fifteen-year-old upcoming player, it was a huge deal to play alongside him and have a shot at winning a medal.

On the court, before we knew it, Lee and I were in the medal rounds. Leander has amazing reflexes which are among the sharpest in the world and we beat the top seeds, Shinobu Asagoe and Thomas Shimada of Japan, 6-3, 6-3 in the first round. The start of the match though, just walking out for the first time to play for my country, in the company of Leander Paes, already a legend of Indian tennis, was nerve-racking. I remember thinking to myself, no matter what happens, no matter how I play, if we lose, it will be because of me. I was the weaker link, I reminded myself. And that thought itself was debilitating. Leander could not play badly.

But Leander has the knack of making you feel extremely comfortable on the court. As his partner, he ensured that I did not feel inferior in any way and that helped me play as best as I could. He was at the top of his game at the time, and together we got the better of Vittaya Samrej and Tamarine Tanasugarn of Thailand in three sets to assure ourselves of a medal.

In the semi-final though, we went down to Yen-Hsun Lu and Janet Lee of Taipei in a tight encounter and had to be content with a bronze. But getting my hands on that medal in the mixed doubles even before I had turned sixteen was thrilling. Winning a medal for my country was a dream come true. I was the youngest medal winner in that edition of the Games across all disciplines.

India had a decent haul of medals in tennis in Busan, winning a gold, a silver and two bronzes. Leander and Mahesh won a gold in the men's doubles and the latter combined with Manisha Malhotra to bag the silver in the mixed doubles, though they lost in the final to the same Taipei pair who beat Leander and me in the semis. Mustafa Ghouse and Vishal Uppal added another bronze in the doubles to the one Leander and I had won in mixed doubles to make it a fairly successful effort by the Indian tennis team at the Asian Games.

I enjoyed the camaraderie with the rest of the team. We would all go out together for dinner in the evenings. Everyone was much older than me, except for Ankita Bhambri and Isha Lakhani, who were closer to my age. I was travelling by myself for the first time and it was exciting to be out and about as a group, supporting our hockey players and fellow Indians competing in other disciplines.

I was extremely high on confidence when I returned from Busan to play the Under-18 Asian Championships in New Delhi. I entered the final with ease and came up against Ankita Bhambri in the battle for the title. I believe it was a worthy contest between two competitive players. We were known to be the brightest emerging stars in the country and we both lived up to our billing that day. Ankita was a very talented player and I sometimes feel sad that she did not go on to achieve what I thought she could have. We were not best friends but I always respected her as a player.

I got the better of her in the summit clash in front of the home crowd – a win that stamped my authority on the court. The singles title made me the first Indian girl to be crowned the Junior Asian Champion. It served to convince me that I was indeed very good at what I was doing.

The season was winding down perfectly, but there was one important pit-stop before my breakthrough year at the national level could come to an end. In December, the National Games would be held in Hyderabad, my home city. The excitement was palpable in the entire state of Andhra Pradesh. Chief Minister Chandrababu Naidu was taking a keen interest in the Games and there was a lot of fanfare all around.

I was No. 2 in the country, and now sixteen years of age. With the restrictions on the number of events I could play as a junior, I was finding it difficult to rise further up in the rankings. Manisha Malhotra was the top player and had been roped in to represent my state of Andhra Pradesh. It created a slight flutter internally in the tennis circle that Hyderabad had decided to import a player from another state. Perhaps there were still doubts about my ability to carry the team on my young shoulders. But on the court, Manisha, a Mumbai based player, and I made a formidable combination.

That was the first time I saw crowds fill the Hyderabad stadium to the brim. The world-class facility, constructed specially for the Games, was jam-packed as huge crowds came out to watch us play. The 6,000-strong audience was not disappointed.

We won the gold in the women's team championship and dominated the play on court. We beat Delhi, represented by the Bhambri sisters, in the quarter-final to start off our campaign. Manisha got the better of Rushmi Chakravarthi while I defeated the battle-scarred veteran, Sai Jayalakshmi, in the semi-final against Tamil Nadu before we outplayed Karnataka in the final to bag the gold. I had another good win over Archana Venkatraman while Manisha quelled the challenge of Sheetal Gautam.

But it was in the singles event that I really asserted myself. I overcame Sheetal 6-2, 6-3 in the first round and outplayed Kolkata's Priyanka Parekh 6-1, 6-0. I went on to overcome Sonal Phadke (who had beaten the top seed, Rushmi Chakravarthi) by an identical margin. This win assured my team of a gold and a silver medal in the women's singles event as my teammate, Manisha, had also come through to the final.

Expectations were high from the final clash – two players who had played alongside in the team event and won the gold now faced each other in the singles final. However, the championship match turned out to be a completely one-sided affair as I played one of the better matches of my life to demolish Manisha en route to a 6-0, 6-0 win. I had won the women's singles gold medal by beating the cream of Indian tennis for the loss of just two games from the quarter-final stage.

This was the first time I had played in front of a packed arena. Having the home crowd rooting for me at every point, all the way, was overwhelming and exhilarating at the same time.

The title established my position as the premier women's tennis player of India at the age of sixteen, giving me the confidence required to make my presence felt at the international level in the months and years that followed.

*

I travelled to Benin City, Nigeria in February 2003 and the trip proved to be a rewarding one as I won both the $10,000 singles titles on African soil to add to my growing confidence. I was in a very positive frame of mind when I caught the flight for Mumbai. However, I was in for a rude shock when I landed at the Sahar International Airport. My mother and I were stopped at the exit point by an official who claimed to be from the Health Department for Control of Yellow Fever. I believed that the dreadful disease was long eradicated and had no idea that I needed to be vaccinated before leaving for the African country. This was infuriating. If this killer disease was still a danger, the Nigerian Embassy could surely have warned us before stamping my visa!

Since we did not have the required papers to show that we had been immunized for yellow fever, we were quarantined in a remote place in the outskirts of the city of Mumbai for five days. We could hardly believe what was happening as my mom and I were whisked away by unknown men in a special car to a huge, depressingly old and ancient looking monument. The irony was dreadful. This bungalow that was to be our quarantine for yellow fever had yellow doors, windows, walls and beds! I remember praying for the doctors to come soon and declare us free of the disease.

Mom called up Dad, who was in Hyderabad, to inform him of

the situation and he immediately flew down to Mumbai. To be fair, the officials tried to make us as comfortable as they could, given the limited budget they seemed to have. But my mother was livid. 'Why are passengers not checked before they board the flight to Nigeria? Why should you even allow people to travel to that country without confirming that they have the immunization certificate if there is a risk of infection?' she questioned the doctor who was in charge of looking after us.

'Our department has been in existence for decades now and we need to go according to the rules since we have been employed specially for this purpose,' was his dubious, unconvincing answer. 'Madam, you will be glad to know that we have quarantined several famous people and celebrities as we want to protect everyone from this terrible disease.' We didn't even know what to say!

We spent the next five days lazing about. News had leaked to the media and our phones rang continuously as the press tried monitoring my health. We spent time playing cards or carrom in the 'yellow house' and I read books and magazines for most of the day. There was no television and the days seemed like weeks. It was a huge relief when we were finally cleared of any risk of having contracted yellow fever and were allowed to go back to the comforts of home and civilization.

9

FIRST BRUSH WITH STARDOM

TWO WINTERS HAD passed since my first steps on the famed courts of Wimbledon.

I was making rapid strides at the Under-18 level, doing well in singles and doubles in the ITF tournaments. But I had failed to create anything more than a ripple in the Junior Grand Slams. When I reached London to prepare for Wimbledon in June 2003, not much was expected of me. In fact, I was still looking for a doubles partner.

When you first hit the tour, it can be a very lonely place. You are young and shy to begin with. I didn't know a lot of people on the circuit and it was difficult for me to break the ice. At the junior level, players tend to travel with their country mates in a close huddle – speaking the same language, sharing the same culture – and it can be difficult for an outsider to break through.

So there I was, all alone, doing what I had always dreamt of – playing with the best upcoming youngsters of the world at the Junior Grand Slams, the breeding ground for future tennis stars. I understood even then that I was with the icons of tomorrow. But no one on the circuit knew me or much about India. They had not seen many Indian girls at that level before and everyone was a little wary. I was an unfamiliar, unknown commodity.

As an extremely shy girl myself, I was partly to be blamed for not really going out and talking to the other girls who were of my age. My parents would often push me to talk to people and make friends, but I was not to be budged from my corner.

The first order of business was to actually find a partner to play with. I had partnered fellow Indian Sanaa Bhambri at the French Open just a month ago and reached the semi-final for a great result. Mahesh Bhupathi had come to watch that match. He told me after we lost in the semis, 'I hope you are not playing together at Wimbledon.' I was furious. Here I was in the semi-final of a Grand Slam and the man was telling me not to play with my partner.

'Why?' I asked him, irritated.

'I don't think you should play with her,' he said and walked off.

It was only later, when we talked about it again, that he explained to me the technical reasons why he thought I should play with someone else, particularly on grass. I decided to follow his advice. When I informed Sanaa about my decision, she was surprised.

As I entered the gates of the famed Wimbledon grounds, I didn't have the safety net of already having a partner and that added to the drama at the biggest Grand Slam of them all. The signs seemed ominous.

The following day, I happened to see Alisa Kleybanova of Russia practising. She had powerful and easy-flowing backhand strokes, which I felt could complement my forehand adequately. There was no time to lose. Despite my shy nature, I walked up to her and asked her to partner me.

Initially, Alisa seemed very hesitant to play doubles. She said she wanted to concentrate on her singles and I went around earnestly looking for someone else to partner. The next morning, though, she walked up to me while I was at practice and said matter-of-factly, 'Sania, I'll play with you if you still haven't found yourself a partner.'

Alisa had concentrated purely on her singles till then and did not boast a very high doubles ranking but I felt confident that we both had the game to go deep into the draw. However, there were to be a few more hiccups before we finally got onto the match courts to battle it out for the most prestigious title in girls' tennis.

*

It was a wet English summer. Rain played havoc with the schedule that year and matches were postponed with monotonous regularity. Finally, under pressure to complete the tournament in time, the organizing committee decided to cut the girls' doubles draw in half! The draw of thirty-two would now be reduced to sixteen. This was going to be problematic for us.

With Alisa's low doubles ranking, we would now struggle to make the cut and she offered to withdraw so that I could play with a higher ranked partner to assure myself of a spot. But I decided to stick with the young Russian and we just about made it to the truncated draw, as the final team to get in.

Our prospects did not seem encouraging at all. We were to meet the top-seeded pair of Jarmila Gajdosova and Andrea Hlavackova in the very first round. So far, nothing had gone according to plan.

I remember my father telling me encouragingly, 'Sania, this is a great opportunity. If you can get past the first round, I think you have a very good chance of winning the title, and if you do, you will climb to the No. 1 spot in the world in girls' doubles rankings.' That was quite a few leaps into the future.

But sport can be a funny business. Extraordinary things happen almost routinely. We spend a lot of time looking at statistics, form, experience and then, on a given day, all calculations can come tumbling down like a pack of cards. It's difficult to predict anything accurately. Top seeds lose, rank outsiders go deep, underdogs win and champions are defeated. And of all sports, perhaps tennis is the most unpredictable.

Alisa and I combined beautifully in our first match together and beat the top seeds 7-6, 6-4. Flushed with success, we continued to win, beating Emma Laine and Nadja Pavic easily, 6-1, 6-2, before surprising a tough American team of Allison Baker and Iris Ichim 6-3, 5-7, 6-4 in the semi-final. Almost miraculously, we found ourselves in the final, as my father had predicted. It was a heady experience. Everything seemed to be happening too fast for us to comprehend and the whole run-up to the final was a bit of a blur.

While we were racking up wins on the court, we were experiencing many firsts off it. There was lots to get used to. Wimbledon is legendary for its traditions and we needed to quickly soak in everything – like walking into the senior locker rooms for the first time. At Wimbledon, juniors are given a separate locker room till they enter the semi-finals and it was an unforgettable moment, entering the special place that is reserved for the pros.

It was a classic rite of passage. Get into the last four and play like the big girls. Before our semi-final, as we prepared for our match, we were in the same space, enclosed by the same walls, with the same pictures, the same ground on which were the same benches that our idols had walked around and sat on. It gave the whole experience an indefinable edge. Like a sneak peek into the future to egg you on, a clear tangible incentive to get into the big league.

After our semi-final win, a day before the final, we were asked to choose the clothes we would wear to the legendary Champions' Ball. An expertly curated wardrobe was brought into the locker room. Racks of stunning dresses, shoes and handbags. Growing up, I had heard of the Wimbledon Ball, of players letting their hair down and dancing. It was almost unfair to do this to the players a day before they were to play the final! We were already dreaming of strutting our stuff at the ball. We selected our clothes and went to bed that night, looking forward to the biggest day of our lives.

Our final was against Katerina Bohmova and Michaella Krajicek, the pair I had lost my French Open doubles semi-final to earlier that year. The Wimbledon title clash was definitely a revenge match for me.

Nerves were rampant as we entered the court. My partner, Alisa, had played splendidly so far. But she was even younger than I was, all of thirteen, and finding it difficult to hold her nerve in her first

Wimbledon final. I knew I had to be the calm one, though I myself was playing for my first Grand Slam title. I decided to take the initiative and control play. It seemed to work as we came back from a set and a break down to take the final into the decider.

I distinctly remember the championship point. I told myself that I would not take any chances and would concentrate on keeping the ball in play from the baseline. I engaged the rival duo in a long rally, finally forcing a feeble lob from our opponents which Alisa, at the net, needed to barely tap in for a winner.

She went for the kill but, in her anxiety, totally mistimed the stroke. The ball hit the top of her racket frame and sailed over our opponents' heads. But it landed inside the baseline for an impossible winner. Game, set, match and Wimbledon championship to Miss Sania Mirza and Miss Alisa Kleybanova!

The whole of India erupted! It was the first time ever that an Indian girl had won at Wimbledon and the achievement was celebrated with excitement and fanfare all over the country.

I came home to a rousing reception in Hyderabad and was driven in an open-top jeep from the airport to be congratulated by Chief Minister Chandrababu Naidu at his home and Governor Surjit Singh Barnala at Raj Bhavan. Thousands of supporters along with dozens of media persons and officials joined the procession that had the city of Hyderabad gleaming with pride.

For the next few months, the media just would not tire of me and I was followed relentlessly wherever I went. Some of the newsmen almost camped in my house, devising new ways and means of presenting me. One image that the media took a particular liking for and played up all the time was that of a young, brash party-goer who also happened to play tennis. I had always liked dressing up from my childhood days. I knew I was reasonably presentable and enjoyed wearing clothes that I felt suited me. But I had never been very outgoing, and the description of me as a fashion-conscious party girl could not have been more off the mark.

However, that was just a small bother as I was busy soaking in the smiles of joy on the faces of fellow Indians wherever I went for the next few weeks. I was thrilled when Sachin Tendulkar arranged for his signature Fiat Palio car to be presented to me. Though he could not attend the function that was organized by the Jubilee Hills Club in Hyderabad to felicitate me for the Wimbledon win, he telephoned me at the precise moment and congratulated me for my achievement. I think I was more excited about receiving his call than I was on being given the keys to the prized car!

Crowds thronged in huge numbers to the felicitation and celebratory functions arranged in Hyderabad and in several other Indian cities – on the streets, at the airports, almost everywhere. Perhaps the country had been desperately in need of a female sporting icon and I was filling that vacuum. It was my first glimpse of superstardom and I felt humbled by the experience.

10

THE GOLD RUSH AND BEYOND

I STILL HAD more than a year left to play in the junior circuit, if I so desired. But having already claimed the coveted No. 1 spot in the world in girls' doubles and with a Wimbledon title under my belt, I wasn't inclined to pursue my juniors' career any more. I had also achieved a ranking of No. 10 in singles. Tough decisions needed to be made and following careful deliberation, I decided to stop playing the junior tournaments after September and concentrate on the professional women's circuit instead.

The Afro-Asian Games were to be hosted by Hyderabad in October 2003 and there was plenty of excitement and enthusiasm being generated all over the country. The success of the National Games held the previous year had given a fillip to sports in Hyderabad and raised expectations from it as a sporting destination. The infrastructure that had been painstakingly built for the National Games was tidied up to meet international standards.

I met Chief Minister Chandrababu Naidu a few days before the Games. 'The country is expecting a lot from you, Sania,' he said to me. The chief minister had provided ample support to me through the offices of the Sports Authority of Andhra Pradesh and I thought to myself that perhaps this was my chance to justify the faith that he and his team had reposed in me in the past. 'I'll try my very best, sir,' I assured him with a smile.

In fact, I went a step further. I had the most amazing week of tennis at the Afro-Asian Games. I didn't lose a single match and won four gold medals with a victory in every event that I participated in.

Rushmi Chakravarthi and I represented India in the team event and after an easy tie against Nigeria, we scripted thrilling singles wins against the Indonesian players, rendering the doubles redundant. We both won our singles matches via a third set tie-break to pocket the gold for India. While Rushmi beat Septi Mende, I quelled the challenge of Sandy Gumulya 7-5 in a nail-biting tie-breaker that had the crowds on the edge of their seats.

In the women's singles individual event, I started off with a fluent victory over Fadzai Mawisire of Zimbabwe and got the better of Czarina Arevalo of Philippines in the semis. The final was an all-Indian affair where I beat Rushmi in straight sets for the gold.

Rushmi and I won the women's doubles as well and I combined with Mahesh Bhupathi in the mixed doubles to annex my fourth gold medal for India. All in all, it turned out to be a memorable week for me and I emerged as the highest gold medal winner of the Games in any discipline. The home crowd made the whole experience even sweeter.

This was my first tournament in India after having won the Wimbledon girls' doubles crown and it was a great feeling to live up to the huge expectations of my country while playing at home. In his concluding speech, the chief minister spoke about the promise I had made to him before the start of the Games – that I would try my best to win gold for India – and how proud he was that I had kept my word.

In 2004, I continued to win ITF titles at the $10,000 level in various countries all over the world as I focused on improving my professional women's ranking. I was the champion in Boca Raton (USA) and then in Rabat (Morocco), Campobasso (Italy), Wrexham and Hampstead (England) before going on to win my first $25,000 title in August in New Delhi.

My trip to Nigeria two months later for a couple of Challengers proved to be another memorable experience. I won both the $25,000 titles in Lagos but the conditions were far from comfortable. There were unconfirmed reports of gunshots being fired nearby and we preferred to stay in the confines of our hotel as much as possible. Security was a major concern and going to restaurants was not a viable option, given the tense atmosphere. My mother would accompany a couple of armed guards to the market every day to buy groceries and she cooked for us outside our room. This was economical and safe and became popular with the girls and boys who were also playing in a Challenger tournament simultaneously in the same city. Pakistan's top player, Aisam-ul-Haq Qureshi and his coach, Robert Davis, still remember the food that my mom dished up in unusual circumstances.

Every single step of the ladder in the world of professional tennis is a great education in itself and one learns so much through travel to different corners of the world. I may have missed out on a lot of classes while travelling for tournaments and I didn't learn too much history or geography from books. However, I did play tennis on courts overlooking the pyramids in Egypt and I did get the opportunity to visit several other historic destinations of the world. I feel privileged to have experienced so many different cultures while meeting all kinds of people from various countries. No amount of studying in classrooms could have given me such an education.

11

OF COACHES AND CRITICS

I TURNED PROFESSIONAL in 2003 but the year of ascension, if I may call it that, was 2005. Not only did I shine in the Australian Open on my Grand Slam debut but also won a WTA singles title in Hyderabad soon after and went on to beat the reigning US Open champion in Dubai. The events of that defining year changed my life forever.

Of course, it wasn't just my own efforts that took me places. I am always quick to acknowledge the hard work of the coaches who trained me long before I became a well-known name in India and beyond.

Looking back, I can say that I have had the good fortune to work with some of the most brilliant and respected coaches in the world. However, I was a bit unlucky that I did not get the opportunity to train with them in the early, formative years of my career. That way I could have avoided some of the technical flaws in my game which they collectively smoothened out at various stages, to some extent, but could not totally eliminate.

Mahesh Bhupathi's father, C.G.K. Bhupathi, was the first senior coach I worked with, although very briefly. He watched me play my debut match at Wimbledon in 2001 and was impressed with my game and temperament but believed my backhand needed a lot of work. He was also the first coach to point out that my technique of dropping the elbow while serving needed immediate correction.

I was in my mid-teens when I went for a fortnight to the Bhupathi

Tennis Village in Bengaluru to work on specific aspects of my game. My new coach helped me improve my backhand but after having tried for a week to straighten out the elbow problem in my serve, suggested that it might be too late to rectify that particular shortcoming. He proved to be right because even in later years, some of the best coaches could only come up with a compromise rather than a complete solution to my problem.

It was C.G.K. Bhupathi who suggested a stint for me with the renowned Bob Brett. I travelled to the Australian maestro's academy in San Remo, the beautiful seaside resort in northern Italy. Isha Lakhani and Megha Vakharia also joined me at Bob Brett's Tennis Academy and for the first time in my life I witnessed the work ethic of a top-class international coach.

Bob Brett was a purist and a workaholic. He was a perfectionist when it came to imparting technique and I am yet to come across someone as meticulous as he was in that respect. We would play tennis for five hours a day and then train hard for a couple more hours. The physical training was methodical and extremely tough on the body. By the end of the week, we were sore as sore could be.

Vedran Martic, a Croatian friend of Bob, happened to be at the Academy during one of my stints. They had worked together as part of Goran Ivanisevic's tour team. As a tennis coach, I think Vedran was a genius in his own right. It was he who modified my backhand in the span of a week and my game immediately went up a few notches. He also worked on my serve and filmed my action in slow motion to understand the problem before analysing it.

I learned to volley a bit – not to Bob's satisfaction, I'm afraid, but at least I was improving. Bob and Vedran tried hard to improve the position of my elbow on the serve, but after a while they gave up. They felt it was too late to eliminate the technical flaw that was to hurt me all through my career. 'You would have to maybe stop playing tournaments for at least a year, work on completely reconstructing the serve and then at the end of it all, there is no guarantee that the new serve will be better,' Bob explained. If only this simple problem had been diagnosed and corrected earlier, when I was still young and learning to play, I could have had a much better serve.

The best coaches in the world believe that after the age of fourteen it becomes very difficult to change the position of the dropped elbow on the serve. All I could do was try, and that I've done for years, ever since I turned sixteen, which is when it was first pointed out to me.

'Sania undoubtedly has some talent but she has plenty of weaknesses in her technique,' Bob explained to my father, when I was still playing in the junior category. 'If she works on these weaknesses and everything else falls into place, she can perhaps achieve, at best, a world ranking of No. 30 in professional women's tennis.' At that time, even breaking into the magical top-100 seemed far-fetched to me and to all the people my father mentioned this to. But Bob Brett isn't regarded as highly as he is for no reason. His judgement was almost accurate and I was happy to go a few steps further, achieving a career-best singles ranking of No. 27 in the world.

It was much later that I also had the opportunity of working with Australian legend Tony Roche, John Farrington from the Bahamas, Spaniard Gabriel Urpi, Dutchman Sven Groeneveld and Rob Steckley of Canada. I should also add the names of Akhtar Ali, the former Indian Davis Cup coach, and Frenchman Christian Filhol, who were always forthcoming with advice and encouragement whenever I needed it.

When I first hit the headlines in world tennis, I think I had a dangerous forehand that shocked my opponents into temporary submission. However, I lacked a reliable, effective serve, my backhand was frail, my volleying skills were non-existent, my movements were sluggish, my fitness level inadequate for top-flight tennis and I was short of a meaningful strategy in my game.

But after making it to the higher echelons of the sport, especially when I broke into the top-100 largely on the back of one major strength which was my forehand, I had to suffer the ignominy of working on my several weaknesses in the full glare of public scrutiny in order to survive at that level. I also had to attempt to make these changes and improvements in my game without taking any major breaks and do it quickly enough to prevent my world-class opponents from destroying and banishing me from the Grand Slam level forever.

All the professional coaches who saw me at close quarters at different stages of my career understood the reasons for the technical and physical limitations in my game and worked towards finding alternative solutions, using all the experience and expertise that they had at their disposal. However, the majority of the inexperienced club-level coaches who watched me from a distance and some of my staunchest and most valued supporters felt frustrated by my inability to break into the top-10 in singles, which is where they felt my forehand belonged.

I knew I could not expect my fans to fully comprehend the problems that I struggled with. I was just immensely grateful to them for the love and high regard they showed for my game and for me all through my career. What they may not have realized is that I was actually harsher on myself than they could ever be. I expected more out of me than anyone else did and my coaches knew that.

I never shirked hard work and if I had not improved substantially upon all those weaknesses that I had when I broke into the elite group, I know I would have been blown out of the top-100 within weeks. What disappointed me was the scorn directed at me by some critics, on account of my not being able to develop a good enough serve to win a Grand Slam in singles or not improving my fitness to match a natural athlete like, say, Elena Dementieva. They attributed it to a lack of effort and ambition on my part. This was simply not true and I have to admit that I found it hard to digest the fact that some people who claimed to be my well-wishers publicly questioned my commitment to a sport that is my life, without bothering to make any attempt to understand the underlying nuances.

There were some critics who felt I should not have changed coaches so many times and should have stuck to one. I do not agree. There are no clear-cut rules that frame the success of a professional tennis player. What works for one may not suit another. While there are instances of players having done well by working with the same coach for years, there have also been several successful players who had different coaches at different times in their career. Roger Federer, for instance, has had stints with a few coaches including Tony Roche, Stefan Edberg and Ivan Ljubicic among others. All through his career, Rafael Nadal has worked with his uncle, Tony, who has not produced another player of calibre, besides his phenomenal nephew. The Williams sisters preferred hitters to full-time coaches for a long while and former World No. 1 Caroline Wozniacki used the services of her father, Piotr, who was a soccer player and had never played tennis in his life. Then there's Wimbledon champion Marion Bartoli, who was coached for a major part of her career in the most unorthodox manner by her father, Walter Bartoli, who happened to be a medical doctor.

Perhaps what worked for me even while I was changing coaches at regular intervals was that my father remained a constant figure who continued to be hands-on with each of the professionals I trained with. He ensured that there was continuity and equilibrium in the way the game was taught to me by the various coaches – each of them skilled and renowned in their own way.

I got along well with every coach I worked with and developed a special rapport with each of them. C.G.K. Bhupathi was considered to be very strict on court by his students but I would joke with him (as I did with all my other coaches). This surprised and even shocked some of the other boys and girls at his academy. However, I believe I knew where to draw the line.

I remember reading a quote from him in a newspaper, where he admitted how he much he had enjoyed coaching me. 'Sania brought in an element of fun on the court even when she was working seriously,' he said. 'She was mischievous, yet respectful, and had the audacity to joke with me. She was spirited on the court and carried the coach-student relationship to a wonderful level that I had not shared with any other player I had worked with!'

Bob Brett and I shared a similar rapport and I do hope he enjoyed working with me. Straight after one of my stints with him at his

12

MY GRAND SLAM DEBUT

MY PROFESSIONAL WOMEN'S ranking had improved dramatically by 2004. However, I was still some distance away from the top-100 mark that would give me a chance to play in the Grand Slams in the women's category. In order to speed up the process, I competed in the Asian Championship in Tashkent – the winner there was to be rewarded with a wild card into the main draw of the Australian Open. I did reach the final, where I lost to China's Li Na and felt terribly disappointed at having missed out on a golden opportunity.

Then things began to happen. Li Na struck a purple patch in her career and went into a destructive spree, annihilating virtually every opponent who came her way. She improved her ranking quickly and substantially to get a direct entry into the main draw of the Australian Open. This opened a window of opportunity for me as I was the next in line to be granted the wild card as the losing finalist of the Asian Championship. And so, by a strange twist of fate, I found myself in the main draw of the Australian Open.

*

Mom and Dad had decided in September 2004 to undertake the Haj to Mecca in December-January. My parents were convinced that it was the blessings of their intention of performing the 'once-in-a-lifetime' pilgrimage that had clinched the issue as far as my debut in a Grand Slam was concerned.

But the dates of the pilgrimage that year overlapped with those of the Australian Open. My mother's dear friend, Neela Aunty, offered to escort me to my first professional Grand Slam and her daughter Anuja, who is a good friend of mine, accompanied us. While my parents prayed in Mecca, I created a few waves Down Under in the summer of 2005.

Cindy Watson of Australia was my first opponent as I made my Grand Slam debut in the women's category of the Australian Open. I was nervous at the start and lost the first set easily. I seemed to be going down tamely in the second before striking some good form. I not only outplayed Cindy from that point but also went on to beat Petra Mandula 6-2, 6-1 in the second round after she had knocked out Flavia Pennetta – the seed in my part of the draw – in her previous match.

This set up a third-round match against Serena Williams and everyone in India was beginning to get excited. I was thrilled to be playing against someone of Serena's stature but I was anxious as well. I remember Mahesh Bhupathi coming up to me before the match and telling me, 'San, go out there, enjoy yourself and give it your best shot. Even if you are outplayed by one of the greats of the game, you will neither be the first nor the last in women's tennis history to suffer at the hands of Serena Williams!'

The Indian media was now getting totally involved and my phone was buzzing endlessly. My parents were at this time in the city of Mina in the middle of their pilgrimage, completely out of touch with what was going on in Melbourne. They had no idea that I had won my second round at the Australian Open and was soon going to play the most important match of my life till then.

Dad had silenced the ringtone of his cellphone. When he did accidentally glance at it while having lunch in the group tent, he was taken aback to see more than a hundred missed calls from strange Indian numbers. With Anam fending for herself at home in

Hyderabad, he was naturally alarmed and immediately picked up the cellphone to answer the next call. It was from an excited television correspondent, who conveyed the news of me going head-to-head against Serena Williams in the third round of the Australian Open and requested him for a reaction.

'Thank you for giving me the news but I am in the middle of the desert in Saudi Arabia, performing Haj amongst millions of other pilgrims and there is no way you can find me here,' Dad explained.

The media man, however, had other ideas. 'One of our correspondents is also performing the pilgrimage,' he said. 'If you can give me your location, he will find you and get your live reaction!'

My father declined. 'I am sorry,' he said. 'This is one time you will have to excuse me, sir. The Australian Open is hardly the most important thing on my mind at this moment!'

*

Standing on the other side of the net against Serena Williams, with the world watching, would have been a daunting task for any eighteen-year-old and I felt the load of expectations of my entire country on my shoulders. I struggled to hold my own against a rampaging Serena and was down 0-5 before I even knew what hit me. It was only then that I could get on the scoreboard with my first game of the match, relieved at having avoided the ignominy of being bageled. I remember smiling to myself at that point and raising my hands in personal triumph. I looked up at the players' box from where Neela Aunty and my cousins, Hina and Husna, stared anxiously at me.

But I had settled down a bit now and was beginning to find my feet, exhibiting some confidence and playing a few scintillating strokes that had Serena scampering desperately round the court. The crowd warmed up to me and I enjoyed showing off my skills. I thought I played well and lost 4-6 in the second set, beaten but not disgraced. The great champion that she is, Serena had some genuine words of encouragement for me as we shook hands at the end of the match. They meant a lot to me.

I wrapped up a good campaign, satisfied at having made it to the third round in my Grand Slam debut and losing only to the world's best. But nothing could have prepared me for what I was to experience on my return home. It was the start of a new life under the unrelenting gaze of the media and the public.

I came home from Melbourne to another hero's welcome. This time the scale was bigger than anything I could have imagined. I was taken aback by the amount of coverage my third round at the Grand Slam had received and by the number of people who were at the airport to receive me. The media was in near hysteria, a state that has become quite common in recent years with its ever growing presence, reach and numbers.

My parents arrived from Mecca just a few hours before my flight touched down in Hyderabad and they joined in the celebrations. There were big banners put up on the roads leading to my house from the airport. My encounter with a tennis giant like Serena Williams on almost level terms had excited people back home and they greeted me with the warmth reserved for champions. I was overwhelmed!

The Australian Open in 2005 was like a massive explosion in my life. It filled it with hope, belief and immense possibilities. It also opened up a barrage of public support and scrutiny that has simply not subsided since then. The next two weeks whizzed past and I can recall very little of that time. All I remember is doing one interview after another and being followed everywhere, each time I stepped out of my house. Even before I could understand and come to terms with what was happening, the turn my life was taking, or rather had taken, it got bigger and bigger. If the Australian Open was the big bang of my universe, the next event became the first turning point in its burgeoning and expanding story.

13

CHAMPION AT HOME

THE THIRD WTA tournament in my hometown of Hyderabad was my next target. I had been given a wild card the two previous years but failed to win a round in singles. I thought I had played well on both occasions but lost in three sets to the Aussies, Eva Dominicovic in 2003 and Nicole Pratt, who was the winner in 2004. I had won the doubles title though, with Liezel Huber, which was another first for an Indian woman.

But I desperately wanted to do well in singles. I believed my game had improved considerably since the last time I played here and with a little bit of luck, I knew I could upset a few of my more accomplished opponents. All through my career I'd had a wonderful record in Hyderabad. I had won several AITA tournaments, the $10,000 ITF event as well as the Hyderabad Open doubles title the previous year and I felt that the WTA singles trophy would be the icing on the cake – a tribute to my home city and the lovers of tennis who had given me immense support all through these years.

The legendary Martina Navratilova had come down for this tournament to play doubles and was to be its showpiece. Unfortunately, her German partner, Anna-lena Groenefeld, injured herself and Martina was forced to forfeit her match early in the tournament.

With a singles ranking of 131, I needed a wild card to get into the main draw and I would have to upset every opponent I was pitted against in order to move up in the tournament. Naturally, they were all ranked higher than me. I was drawn to meet Delia Sescioreanu of Romania in the first round and played solid tennis to out-hit her, scoring a morale-boosting 6-2, 7-5 victory. The home crowd loved every minute of it and backed me all through the match.

Zheng Jie of China was my next opponent. Very few gave me any chance against this Chinese girl who had been performing consistently. However, with a victory under my belt, I felt a lot more confident as I went into the match. I started with some big shots that took Zheng by surprise and before she could settle down, I had pocketed the first set.

She used her experience to slow the game down in the second set even as I became more and more error-prone, allowing her back into the contest. But as the match went into a decider, I was determined to not let go. I continued with my attacking brand of tennis and that paid off handsomely. To the delight of a huge partisan crowd, I won and was through to the quarter-final.

The hysteria was slowly building up around the event and these two wins attracted a considerable following for the tournament all over the country. An even bigger crowd came to the stadium for my quarter-final against the seasoned Israeli veteran, Tzipora Obziler. Top-class tennis was not a regular sight in India back then; India's first WTA event was only in its third year. What was even more exciting for the quality-hungry fans was an Indian woman going deep into the draw with some fantastic wins.

Tzipora, who was almost ten years older than me, was my worst nightmare. She was known to be an absolute grinder, blessed with unbelievable stamina and a will to chase down balls all day. She made very few unforced errors and rarely attempted winners. She was a player who did not give you a rhythm through a shrewd mix of pace and trajectory, slowly and steadily forcing her opponent into committing errors. This was exactly the kind of opponent I hated playing against, particularly at that stage of my career. I went down 4-6 in the first set.

Stung by that early loss, I broke loose, hitting the lines with some fiery shots laced with a tinge of disdain that left Tzipora reeling under the heat of my forehand. Very soon, it was all square at one set apiece and in a nail-biting third set, I came back from the brink, saving a couple of match points before closing out the pulsating quarter-final encounter 7-5 in the tie-break after over three hours of play. As I raised my arms to celebrate, relief took over every muscle in my body.

Tzipora was stunned, left sobbing after her crushing loss. It was one of those matches where both players had left everything on the court. While winning such a contest can become a huge reservoir of faith in your own ability for years to come, a loss can leave you in tatters. The win made me much stronger, physically and mentally, especially since I had played in front of a large crowd with huge expectations. But Tzipora was clearly reeling. She had given it everything, put the very last ounce of her energy into the match, and still lost. That's the sort of thing that can break you if you are not strong enough to come out of it soon.

Later in the locker room she confided to me, 'I thought you were going to go away, but you just did not.'

Tzipora was one of those unlucky professional players who survived on the circuit for well over a decade and yet never managed to win a tour title. Years later, she told me how much that loss in Hyderabad continued to hurt her even after the passage of time. She had truly believed she had the match under her belt.

*

I was now in the semi-final of my home event – it was a first for Indian tennis. The matches were being broadcast live on national television and the excitement generated by a string of victories by a home player was infectious. The demand for tickets at the stadium was going out of control and seats were filling up hours before the matches. Glamour girl Maria Kirilenko of Russia was up next.

Pretty Maria was a popular figure in India, having been the runner-up the previous year. She had shown superb form in this tournament as well, while knocking out top seed Li Na in the quarter-final in straight sets. We played a great match and to the delight of the local fans, I pulled it off in the second set tie-breaker to march into my first ever WTA final.

The expectations of the fans hit the roof. The euphoria had to be seen to be believed. The stadium filled up six hours before the match was to begin, at 9 a.m. in the morning. Thousands continued to wait outside, trying to get in, and the police had a tough time keeping them at bay. Every few minutes, the gates would be pushed open as men, women and children tried to get in, and there would be chaos all around. Even Mahesh Bhupathi, an organizer – his company, Globosport, had conceptualized the tournament – could not get in. Eventually he had to jump a back wall to make it inside.

'Sania, you brought us from cricket to tennis', screamed one interesting banner held up by a group of youngsters in the stands. To be playing a high-profile final in your hometown in front of your own people is the kind of stuff dreams are made of and there I was – living that dream. A special 'Sania Mirza Enclosure' was set up in one part of the stands and about a hundred of my family members, friends and close associates were in it. Several relatives and friends could not get in through the gates despite having valid tickets and decided to go home and catch the excitement on television.

All roads led to the tennis stadium that day and the city virtually came to a standstill. The organizers were eventually forced to release a statement on the local TV channels to request people to watch the match on television and refrain from trying to get into the stadium, which was bursting at the seams.

A huge television screen was hastily set up in the indoor stadium nearby and several of the spectators who were unable to reach the centre court were accommodated there. Even that area quickly filled up as thousands thronged the stadium to get close to the action.

I was to play Aloyna Bondarenko of Ukraine in the final and the match lived up to the occasion. Certainly, we kept the crowd on tenterhooks till the end. We both started out tentatively but the quality of tennis picked up as we settled in. I won the first set 6-4 and

Aloyna came back to win 7-5 in the second. Soon I was up a match point in the decider.

Serving for the championship from the ad court, I could barely hear myself. The stadium seemed to be reverberating. Aloyna missed a return off my second serve and I fell to the ground, bursting with joy. I had done it! I had won my first WTA title.

But the drama was far from over. A few moments later, I realized the umpire had still not called it 'game, set and match'. I looked at the umpire's chair as I got up from the ground and saw that he was calling for a re-serve because, in his opinion, the ball had touched the net.

A loud collective gasp filled the stadium as fans shook their heads in disbelief. It was one of the toughest things I had ever had to do – walk back to the service line after I thought I had won the match. In my head, I had to win it twice over. It wasn't surprising that I lost that service game. But as I settled down again after the initial shock, there was no denying me what I wanted so badly. I broke Aloyna in the next game to finally achieve the cherished victory on home soil.

I was flushed with pride at having been able to keep my wits about me after the fragility of the moment when I thought I had already won. I knew I would have to display mental toughness to not let the match slip from my hands and I didn't let myself down. To have done it in Hyderabad, a year after winning the doubles title, was to my mind an unbelievable achievement.

The stadium erupted and after several minutes of absolute chaos, Chief Minister Y.S. Rajasekhara Reddy handed me the trophy to the utter delight of my home crowd.

*

Everything was falling into place. I had won the Wimbledon Juniors title, then announced my presence at the highest level of the sport in a Grand Slam at the Australian Open. Now I had won a WTA singles title, the first Indian woman ever to do so, and significantly, I would now break into the top-100 of the women's world rankings list. Everyone had been talking about me since I was fifteen, how I was going to be the next big thing in Indian tennis, a women's player unlike any who had come before. A lot of times you hear that kind of talk and in the end, nothing comes of it. It can put a lot of pressure on an upcoming young player to be saddled with huge expectations. But at that moment I thought to myself, 'Oh my god, I am actually doing it.' It was like a fairytale for which some writer had created the perfect script.

We celebrated at the stadium, then at home with Aunt Hamida – my mother's sister – and her family leading the way. She is one of my favourite aunts, almost like my 'second mother' and her excitement on my victory knew no bounds even though she is far removed from the world of sport. Finally, I went over to the party hosted by AITA vice-president Raja Narsimha Rao – a man who had always believed in my abilities and supported me throughout my career. All the office bearers of the Association were beaming with joy and pride. The president of AITA, R.K. Khanna, was there too and he looked like he was on top of the world.

He called me aside. 'God bless you, Sania,' he exclaimed. 'You have given me great joy today. It had always been my dream to have an Indian win a prestigious tennis title in India before a full house. You not only won the title, but you also filled up the stadium, my child. I watched your match on television and the fact that I could not even get inside the stadium because of the huge crowd that came to watch you play makes this one of the happiest days of my life!'

I was overwhelmed with emotion and tears started to well up in my eyes. I tried with all my will to control myself as I gave him a warm hug and he kissed me on my forehead. That was the last time I ever met the grand old man of Indian tennis, for he passed away some months later. However, I still share a healthy relationship with his son, Anil Khanna. A different kind of relationship, because he is much younger and I had become a more established player by the time he took over the reins, but we respect each other. We have had our differences, but they never remained unresolved.

14

LEARNING NEW RESPONSIBILITIES

IMMEDIATELY AFTER WINNING my first WTA title at the Hyderabad Open, I received hundreds of invitations to attend functions as a special guest from all kinds of organizations and individuals. Of course, it was not physically possible to accept more than a few of them but some I felt compelled to attend, such as a fundraising event in Siliguri, which was meant to raise money for the victims of the ravaging tsunami that had shocked the entire world in December 2004.

The then urban development minister of West Bengal, Asoke Bhattacharya, was a man who loved sport. He had invited the Indian cricket captain, Sourav Ganguly, football star Bhaichung Bhutia and myself to his constituency. We were to auction our personal belongings to raise funds for the victims of the tsunami. The respect and love that people in this region have for sportspersons is quite unbelievable and it was a memorable experience, being lavished with that kind of adulation.

Perhaps not many of the sports fans there understood the nuances or finer points of the game of tennis as it is football that remains a dominant craze in West Bengal. However, this did not stop them from taking to the streets in large numbers and thronging the footpaths of Siliguri to catch a glimpse of the emerging tennis player who had just won an international title in Hyderabad, soon after locking horns with

71

Serena Williams at the Australian Open. I was accorded a spontaneous standing ovation as my car made its way down the winding roads of the pretty little town.

Crowds filled the balconies and terraces of the buildings and cottages that we passed on our way to the Kanchenjunga Stadium, where the auction was to be held. Thousands of men, women and children lined the streets and waved excitedly at me during the half-hour drive through the town of Siliguri. Some of them carried banners and placards celebrating my achievements. It was an experience that I can never forget. The kind of following that tennis seemed to have in distant towns of the country was staggering and the impact of my performances on people everywhere was a revelation to me. It re-ignited my own personal resolve to continue to do well, wherever and whenever I played – even if it was only to spread happiness amongst the people of my country.

The Kanchenjunga Stadium was packed to capacity and the memorabilia that Sourav, Bhaichung and I had donated were sold within minutes. The dress that I had worn during my Australian Open duel with Serena Williams fetched a whopping two lakh rupees. It felt good to have played a small part in my own little way in raising funds for the thousands who had been devastated by the tsunami.

We were scheduled to take a train to Kolkata after the event but the crowds in Siliguri refused to budge. Dozens of women from the security forces worked in tandem with their male colleagues to help me virtually 'escape' from the stadium that evening. Thousands lined up on the streets once again as my car sped to the railway station and then I was escorted amidst tight security through a mass of humans, who had virtually taken over the platform. Sourav Ganguly and Asoke Bhattacharya had boarded the train earlier and waved anxiously at me from their compartment. It was almost a relief to finally be on our way when the train made its way out of the platform.

My parents and sister had accompanied me on the trip and we spent an enjoyable hour in the compartment, chatting with Asoke Da and Sourav while nibbling away at the home-cooked food the former had packed for us. As the train chugged its way back to Kolkata, I was left reflecting on the different roles I now had to get used to playing. I was a tennis player to start with, but my success on the courts had given me a status and reach that I felt compelled to use to play an even more important part in helping any cause that genuinely mattered to people in my country. I suddenly felt more grown up and mature than all my fellow eighteen-year-old friends and colleagues.

15

THE BEST MATCH OF MY LIFE

IF I WERE to pick the greatest singles tennis match of my life, it would have to be the second round of the Dubai Duty Free Championship in March 2005, in which I made an unbelievable comeback to turn the tables on the reigning US Open Champion, Svetlana Kuznetsova. It was not just the quality of tennis that I managed to conjure up to come back from a hopeless position but also the unique circumstances that made it one of the greatest wins of my career.

I had been given a wild card in the high-profile tournament and very few had expected me to make any kind of impression against the big girls of women's tennis, notwithstanding the fact that I had won my first WTA title a few weeks earlier to break into the top-100 in the world. I beat Jelena Kostanic in the first round to the delight of the huge expatriate crowd that had come out to support me in Dubai and that set up my second round match against the US Open champ.

I had twisted my ankle during the Hyderabad WTA tournament and was still to recover fully from that injury. I had aggravated it further during my match against Kostanic, but that was never going to stop me from trying to give my best against one of the most celebrated players of women's tennis.

Kuzy started off in great style, hitting winner after winner, and I struggled to win a few points in the first four games. I was down 0-4 and 15-30 when I tripped and rolled over on my already injured ankle.

The pain was excruciating. It looked like the end of the tournament for me. I felt totally dejected as the physiotherapist, who had been called onto the court, shook her head and examined the already swollen ankle.

'I don't think you should play, Sania,' she said. 'The ankle doesn't look good and needs to be treated.'

I turned around to the stands from where my family and support group were watching anxiously. 'I'm throwing in the towel,' I said hopelessly, through my tears.

'See if you can finish the set before you let go, Sania!' my parents called out. 'There's a big Indian crowd out here to watch you play. Try and give them something to cheer about.'

Those words inspired me. I took the pain-killers that the physiotherapist gave me and gritted my teeth as she bandaged my ankle. Ten minutes later, I limped back on court to resume the one-sided encounter.

I decided to go for my strokes since I could not imagine winning too many points by hobbling around the court against the No. 7 player in the world, who was already on the rampage. When I won the fifth game to get onto the board, I heaved a sigh of relief.

A few minutes later, the pills began to work and the pain became more manageable. I suddenly rediscovered the forehand and backhand winners in my repertoire and these continued to flow from my racket as I produced some magical strokes that left the crowd gasping for more. I felt like I had gone into a trance as I stroked the ball fluently and with clinical precision.

The television commentator who had been quick to point out how 'the US Open champion was giving a lesson to the upstart, Mirza' when I was struggling at 0-4, now began to understand that a game of tennis is never over until 'game, set and match'! She was, however, magnanimous enough to accept that, all of a sudden, 'Mirza was using her racket almost like a magic wand while producing unbelievable winners'!

I have watched the video recording of that match against Kuzy several times and on each occasion I have myself been amazed by the quality of my strokeplay on that day in Dubai. Everything I tried seemed to work as ball after ball landed precisely where my racket intended it to fall.

Daniela Hantuchova, who was invited to the commentators' box for her views during the course of the match, opined that I was playing many brilliant strokes but there was no way I could keep that up till the end of the match to topple the US Open champion. As a matter of fact, I did finish the match in style to score my first ever top-10 win. After having been down 0-4 when I twisted my ankle, I dropped just two more games to run away with a stupendous 6-4, 6-2 victory against one of the great players of my era.

However, this was not the only time that I was involved in a memorable encounter against Kuzy. We played another humdinger of a match a few months later, this time on the haloed Centre Court of Wimbledon, and though I ended up on the losing side on that occasion, it proved to be another fiercely competitive, thoroughly absorbing game, worthy of the famed venue where it was played.

I was obviously very excited as soon as I found out that our match had been scheduled for the Centre Court. It was another childhood dream coming true and at that moment, I remembered Dad telling me how his own father had proudly talked to him about the time, decades ago, when he had saved enough money as a student in England to watch a Wimbledon match on Centre Court. How proud my grandfather would have been to watch his son's daughter play on the most famous tennis court in the world. I felt a great surge of love for a grandfather I had not been destined to ever meet. The Centre Court at Wimbledon seemed to forge a strange bond between us that day.

I had beaten Akiko Morigami in a tight three-setter to record my first professional win at Wimbledon and Svetlana was my second round opponent. She was, of course, looking for revenge. I had my chances in the first set as I led 4-2 but Kuzy came back strongly, winning the next four games in a row to take the lead. I then went ahead 3-0 in the second and missed a set-point at 5-3. In a topsy-turvy battle, Svetlana went up 6-5 before I evened the match out by clinching the tie-breaker.

In the decider, she broke me in the third game and then, as I struggled with my serve, she took a commanding 5-2 lead. I did not let up and broke back to 4-5 and had a chance to level the score but Svetlana produced an amazing angle to settle the matter as I took her well out of court on the most critical point of the match.

I came off the Wimbledon Centre Court that afternoon to a standing ovation – disappointed but not disheartened. I knew my grandfather would have been proud of my performance that day.

16

AT THE US OPEN, 2005

EVERY TIME I stepped onto the court, by God's grace, bigger and better things were happening. That was the amazing part of my ascent. The rise was so sudden. I had made the third round of the Australian Open, and then soon after that I won a tournament at home. Then I beat the reigning US Open champion and went on to play a memorable match at Wimbledon. Players often take years to gradually climb these monumental steps in their careers but in my case, there was barely any time for it to sink in. And it was about to get even bigger at the US Open 2005.

Hard courts have always been the surface I am most comfortable on. I like the true, even bounce that helps me take the ball on the rise. The fast pace also helps my brand of powerful stroke play and my results on hard courts over the years are a testimony to this.

Going into the US Open, I already had some momentum behind me. John Farrington travelled with me on tour, starting with the US hard court season of 2005. I was the first female professional tennis player that John coached, having previously travelled on the men's tour, working with the World No. 1 doubles team of Mark Knowles and Daniel Nestor. Mahesh Bhupathi had recommended him to me.

Farrington was a strategist and would talk for hours before and after matches, dissecting various aspects of the game. A wonderful human being, John had been struck down by a major injury and needed a hip replacement surgery just as he was getting into his groove as my coach.

I started my campaign in Cincinnati with a straight-set win over the seventh-seeded German, Anna-lena Groenefeld, before bowing out in the quarter-final. I then qualified for the Stanford WTA tournament, though not without a bit of luck.

I scored a couple of good wins over Canada's Maureen Drake and USA's Lindsay Lee-Waters but lost to Israel's Shahar Peer in the final qualifying round. I was fortunate to be accorded the lucky loser's spot and made full use of that stroke of good fortune by scoring a hard-fought win over the seasoned Greek player, Eleni Daniilidou. That earned me the opportunity to play against Venus Williams for the first time in my life and I enjoyed the experience thoroughly, though the American won in straight sets.

San Diego was next and two straight-set wins over Galina Voskoboeva and Kateryna Bondarenko saw me qualify into the main draw. An easy 6-2, 6-2 victory over top-100 veteran Tathiana Garbin set me up for another high-profile second round match against Nadia Petrova, ranked No. 9 in the world.

I was high on confidence and was playing some inspired tennis. Nadia was a powerfully built girl with one of the biggest serves in the game. But she struggled all through the match against my forehand, which repeatedly perplexed her. I never let her settle down, scoring a facile 6-2, 6-1 victory in the end.

This win over Petrova was significant in more ways than one. Apart from providing the second top-10 victory of my career, it also propelled me into the top-50 in the world and it was another dream come true to be ranked amongst the elite of the game.

My tennis seemed to have caught the eye of at least a few of the greats of the sport. Watching my performance in the Acura Classic at San Diego, tennis legend Pancho Segura, the Ecuador-born American player who roamed the courts in the 1940s and 50s, was reported to have said that my 'hard-hitting game' resembled that of Romanian tennis legend Ilie Nastase.

I was thrilled to be even spoken of in the same breath as Ilie Nastase and by a legendary figure like Pancho Segura! It was a long climb up from the days when the coaches of fellow junior players refused to allow their wards to practise with me because they didn't consider me good enough to be of any use to them.

I had reached the semi-finals in doubles in Cincinnati and the sixteen matches that I had played in a little over a fortnight were beginning to take their toll on me. I faced my old foe Akiko Morigami in the third round in San Diego and was sapped of energy as I went down in three long sets.

My body was tired and I needed a break, but I had to rush to Los Angeles to play in the qualifying draw. I was involved in another tight three-setter, this time against Czech girl Iveta Benesova, and again found myself short of energy at a critical juncture of the match. However, this early loss gave me a full week to recover physically from the hectic schedule and by the time the tournament in Forest Hills got under way, I was well rested.

The historic venue at Forest Hills has an old-world charm about it. This was where the US Open was played for several years before moving to Flushing Meadows, and the aura of the golden past still lingers.

I played Shahar Peer in the first round and avenged my earlier loss to her with a fluent 7-6, 6-1 victory. A couple of straight-set wins against Italian Roberta Vinci and the rising American talent, Alexa Glatch, got me into the second WTA final of my career, where Czechoslovakia's Lucie Safarova awaited me.

We slugged it out for almost three hours before Lucie won 3-6, 7-5, 6-4 and I had to be satisfied with the runner-up trophy. It was anybody's match till the end and I was severely disappointed at missing out on the title. However, the big one was still to be played and I promised myself a good showing in the US Open that was to begin in a couple of days' time, only a few miles away at Flushing Meadows. I needed to use the momentum I had built up to make my mark in the final Grand Slam of the year.

But I still had the ankle injury to contend with. It had never really gone away. At the start of the US Open campaign, eight of my ten toenails were damaged and pain had become a way of life. A stomach pull in the final in Forest Hills had turned into a full-blown tear. You sometimes get greedy as athletes. You don't realize where you need to draw the line. Your body cries out for help but you ignore it. I was playing so well, I just didn't want to stop. I was worried that if I did, it would all go away. I continued playing with huge ankle braces that restricted movement to a great extent but there was no alternative. I had even developed a painful tennis elbow. In my pictures from the US Open that year, I'm all taped up.

My whole arm was taped and my feet too, till the ankles. There was a 3.5 cm tear in my stomach muscle and every time I served, it would get worse. Just a week earlier, the US Open had done the most damage and I felt half broken by the time I reached Flushing Meadows. I would come into the training room two hours early so that I could tape my toes and stick the broken nails in place. Of all the things going on with my body, that was the most painful.

My first-round match was against Mashona Washington. It proved to be a nerve-racking contest, full of ups and downs. John Farrington and my father told me later that watching from the players' box had been traumatic. Mashona and I were both nervous, for different reasons, and the quality of tennis we produced was not very high, but our will to keep fighting made it a thrilling affair. I won the first set tie-breaker 8-6, only to lose the second by an identical score-line. I then broke Mashona and held my serve at a critical point of the third set to record my first win at the US Open. I knew I had won an ugly battle that day, but the fact that I came through was in itself sweet satisfaction. Sometimes victories such as this are more rewarding than the 'prettier' contests.

Maria Elena Camerin of Italy had done me a favour by knocking out the seeded Russian, Dinara Safina, who was in my part of the draw, in the first round. Camerin and I played a better match than my first-round encounter with Mashona but I knew I was not anywhere close to my best. I still did not have a great feel on the ball but kept pushing myself. I overcame a second-set slump to record another win.

Physically, these matches were painful as hell. They were all about mental strength. I was probably risking further injury, but at eighteen you do not think about that. You are just fixated on winning. Later in my career, I grew more conscious of tending to injuries, listening to my body and allowing it to get the rest it needed. But back then, I kept playing and I kept winning. I was hurt but I simply did not want to stop.

Frenchwoman Marion Bartoli was my next opponent and word was spreading quickly that a young Indian girl was playing exciting tennis. Apart from a sizeable contingent of Indians, many locals had begun to follow my matches and I was enjoying their vociferous support.

We did a lot of planning for the Bartoli match. She was an unorthodox player and I needed to play to a plan. Marion had arguably the best pair of hands in women's tennis and was blessed with the gift of controlling the ball by taking it on the rise and virtually on the half volley. This made her a dangerous opponent as she struck the ball very early, taking away valuable reaction time from the opponent. Her hand-eye coordination was unbelievable and the rare style of playing double-handed on both sides made her a very tricky customer to tangle with.

The French girl's weakness was the rather sluggish movement of her feet and that was what I tried to exploit when I faced her in the third round. One or two big shots were never going to win a point against her as she anticipated brilliantly and used her talented hands to put the ball away.

What I needed to do was to build each point by placing a string of strokes to the far corners of the court. Her penchant for playing the forehand with both arms cut down on her reach and made it difficult for her, at times, to reach the away ball. I made her move from one side of the court to the other in order to force errors out of her and in the process, I naturally had to take my chances.

At 4-all in the tie-breaker, I managed to play two brilliant points to change the complexion of the game that had been evenly contested until then. As Marion got aggressive, she had me on the run in both those points until I produced two backhand down-the-line winners on the move that stunned her and won me the first set. I then settled the matter with a 6-4 win in the second.

My body was getting battered with each successive match and pain-killers were my only recourse. The injuries to the stomach muscle, ankle and elbow did not allow me to play at my best and yet I was playing winning tennis. I felt strongly that I would be able to come up with the goods on the big points. My confidence had never been as high and that was the secret of my success as I pulled out the exciting wins that carried me into the last-16 stage of the US Open.

'I never surprise myself,' I told the *New York Times* with the confident exuberance of a teenager after my third-round win. 'I always believed I could do it. It was just a question of when I could do it, and I guess it was sooner rather than later.'

I was carrying on from where I had left off at Wimbledon. And not just on the court. Off the court too, what started at SW19 became a bigger beast for me to deal with.

My interactions in the press room during the tournament, especially with the foreign media, were by and large, fun and cheerfully conducted. The journalists were enjoying their time with me and I enjoyed talking to them. But the fascination with everything I did and wore found me slightly unprepared. If it was the T-shirts at Wimbledon, it turned out to be the nose ring at the US Open. Everything I wore was interpreted as a symbol of rebellion. Maybe it was because the foreign media had never seen a young Indian girl on this stage before. Maybe I just did not fit the American idea of a typical Indian woman.

The nose ring that I had worn since I was very young is a traditional form of jewellery in our part of the world. But for the Western media it was more scandalous than a belly button was at that point of time. Suddenly I found myself answering more questions about my nose ring than my tennis. I thought to myself, 'But my mom used to wear a nose ring. What are you talking about? It's like the most traditional thing an Indian woman can do!'

A section of the media was always looking for something scandalous to report. They found it, no matter how off the mark their portrayal of my nose ring as an ornament of social defiance was. The ring also became a symbol of the cult status I was quickly gaining in public consciousness. It began to be marketed in India as the 'Sania nose ring' and the tiny piece of jewellery became a rage amongst young girls.

Years later, I was the chief guest at an awards ceremony, felicitating young deaf and mute athletes. While the introduction was being made on stage, a translator was using sign language to relay the words to the hearing-impaired children. When my name was announced and I was invited to the podium to address the audience, I saw the translator gesturing to her nose ring as a way of conveying my name. I found it a little strange. The nose ring had become a symbol of my identity itself!

Coming back to the US Open, Maria Sharapova was my opponent in the pre-quarter-final and I was excited to be playing the top seed in the Arthur Ashe stadium. It really is a daunting arena – the tennis venue with the largest spectator capacity in the world – that makes fans in the top rows look like ants when viewed from the court below. It may lack the close-knit charm of a Wimbledon Centre Court but the sheer size of it is incredibly impressive, with the steep aisles rising above your head. The size and theatrical build are intimidating when you first enter the court.

It was a new experience for me – my first year on tour, making the fourth round of the US Open after all the action that had preceded it, playing against a Grand Slam champion like Sharapova. I believe I played a good match but the Russian raised her game a couple of notches as all world-class players do. I stayed in the fight till the sixth game of the first set and then Sharapova exerted her class. The difference between us was probably the serve, and on that day, Maria was not just brilliant but almost flawless in that aspect of her game. I had matched her ground strokes with mine in the rallies but her serve was absolutely top-class. As for me, the loss to her in the pre-quarter-final brought the curtains down on a magical run in the US hard court season of 2005.

17

WITH FAME COMES CONTROVERSY

It was a sunny, breezy Hyderabad afternoon. I was home after having done a few interviews. That seemed to be all I was doing every time I came back from a tennis tour. The Australian Open, winning the Hyderabad title, the victory over Kuznetsova in Dubai, breaking into the top-50, then the US Open fourth round, all of it was keeping me in the media spotlight. I enjoyed it but I also found it extremely exhausting.

I went up to my room on the second floor of our house, hoping to catch twenty minutes to just be with myself until lunchtime. I locked the door and crashed on the bed. Just then, my agent and my mother started knocking incessantly on my door. Initially I tried to ignore their calls, but they would not relent. My mom shouted from behind the door, 'Sania, open up! Come down. The photographer is waiting for you.'

In that moment I felt as though I'd had enough. I just couldn't take it anymore. I started bawling, crying my eyes out like a child. I was tired. I wanted a few minutes alone without having to make small talk with strangers or answering a journalist's questions or looking into a camera. I did not have the energy to fake a smile anymore, to strike a pose or get any make-up done. I had not slept properly in days. All I was doing was answering phone calls – from the media or from my managers. Fame had brought me many pages in the newspapers, many hours on TV channels, and also many sponsorship deals and contracts. But I just wanted a few minutes to relax. Tired to the bone, I had completely forgotten that I had given time for a photoshoot for a magazine. 'I don't want to do the shoot,' I shouted as I buried my face in my pillow.

I lay there crying for a good ten minutes. My family and my agent continued knocking on the door, calling out to me desperately. 'How can you do this? Sania, he has a flight to catch. Come out,' my mother said, trying to coax me into opening the door.

Finally, when I had wept the exhaustion out of me, I felt better again. I knew I could not let the photographer wait any longer or avoid doing the photoshoot with him. It had been planned in advance and I had agreed to the time slot. I collected myself and went downstairs. When I finished the shoot, I was rather pleased with the results. It was done on the balcony of our little garden which offered a wonderful view of my city, with the Charminar – the jewel of Hyderabad – and the Golconda Fort on the horizon.

A few days later, that picture of me adorned a full page of *Time* magazine, which did a special cover story on me. I had been chosen as one of the Asian heroes of 2005.

*

There is no denying the fact that the media played a big role in the recognition I gained for my achievements and for making me the national hero I became after my success in 2005. While it was difficult for me to handle the attention on some occasions, largely because of the pressures on time and personal space, it was also an enriching experience. I have shared a wonderful relationship with most journalists, particularly with the sports scribes. Not many people know that my father was a bit of a sports journalist himself and even published and edited a little magazine in his younger days. And though unusual circumstances took him away from the profession he loved, I think, at heart, he remains a sports writer.

He also has a soft corner for sports journalists and has always ensured that I give them priority if they ever need me for a story. 'Like us, they are in the profession for the love of sport and we share a passion with them,' he says.

I developed a very special rapport with sports journalists early in my career and enjoyed sharing my perspective with them. I think they found me interesting too, and whenever I returned from a successful tour, I loved sharing my success with them. Some of them have known me since I was seven years old and treat me as their own – a feeling that I have reciprocated, rarely denying them time even if it means getting out of bed early in the morning after an exhausting day or answering questions late in the evening to accommodate their deadlines.

Apart from sports writers, I have had a warm relationship with other people in the media too. Many of them have touched my life in the many years that I have been playing tennis. Some of them have gone on to become great family friends and hopefully these relationships will continue to thrive long after I have retired from the game.

However, this does not mean that I have not had arguments or disagreements with some of them. They have been critical of my game, my approach or strategy, especially when I lost a match, and I had no problems with that. Whenever I met them, I would explain my point of view and we would have a healthy discussion on tennis. The one thing that bound us together was our love for the sport.

But earlier in my career, dealing with the media was in itself an education, like tackling a wild beast. It was difficult to turn down requests from reporters, who were often armed with recommendations from influential people known to me or my family. I would oblige as often as I could, but it was impossible to accommodate everyone. Reporters often forgot that my primary profession and focus was tennis and I would have to say no to a request when it hindered my training and preparation.

But the pressure was relentless. Every little inconsequential detail about me and my life started getting reported as journalists sought to find a unique angle that had not yet been written about. If they did not get access to me, they would sometimes just make up a story.

While talking to sports scribes was always pleasurable, I found that I did not quite share the same rapport with some of the lifestyle and fashion writers and the cub reporters from the electronic media. Youngsters, some of them not much older than I was, would thrust their microphones at me nonchalantly, expecting to surprise me into making a comment that could be blown up into a sensational headline.

I loved to be smartly turned out in my personal life but fashion for the sake of glamour was not something I yearned for. However, the glamour quotient was the only aspect some of the glossies were interested in. My achievements on the tennis courts that had brought me into the spotlight were of no interest to them. It was far more lucrative to portray me as a glamorous doll whose only objective was to use sport as a stepping stone to films.

Readers and viewers now began to be fed a diet of sensational stories about me on a regular basis. The moment one reporter from a newspaper, tabloid or news channel touched on something vaguely controversial, others jumped in as well. They would quickly build on the first titbit to create, at times, almost a sadistic narrative. Before one story could run its course, another reporter would come up with a juicy new story and this went on and on.

At times, stray voices of dissent were blown up to appear as though the whole world was against me. Several television cameras would carry footage to millions of viewers of a dozen attention seekers burning my effigy for the most ridiculous of reasons. A friend of mine from the media confided to me one day, 'Sania, right now there is a great demand for news about you. If a rival newspaper carries a story on any topic that we've missed out on, I am pulled up. Please try to keep me informed. I don't want to lose my job.'

I could sympathize with my friend's predicament but few people, if any, seemed to understand what I was going through. It was emotionally draining for me and my family. By irresponsibly twisting and blowing up inconsequential but sensitive issues, a small group of sensation seeking reporters were unwittingly creating a volatile situation where, at one point, even my security became a matter of concern.

The tennis court was not the venue where I was fighting my biggest battles any more. The Kuznetsovas and the Williams were not the only ones I was combating – I had more potent enemies in my own backyard, wielding weapons that seemed to have been created out of thin air!

It was at this difficult point in my career that a few senior media professionals jumped to my rescue. Some of the biggest names in Indian journalism conveyed their support for me and expressed concern at the shocking lack of restraint shown by certain sections of the fourth estate.

The public and personal support of these journalists meant the world to me. It rejuvenated my crumbling faith in a system that seemed cruelly adept at destroying the spirit of a young, ordinary Indian girl who had dared to dream – for herself and for her country.

*

8 September 2005 will always remain etched in my memory because the events of that day virtually transformed the course of my life. That was the day when a 'fatwa' was reported to have been issued against me for the clothes that I wore on the tennis court. The world's perception of me changed overnight.

I received an excited phone call from a friend in the media, asking for my reaction. A Muslim cleric belonging to a religious organization had reportedly issued the fatwa against me in an interview with a journalist of a national newspaper. He had, in fact, said that Islam did not allow women to wear skirts, shorts and sleeveless tops in public, in response to a query posed by the reporter. Excited analysts quickly jumped to their own conclusions. They claimed that the gentleman had threatened to physically harm me for wearing the clothes I did.

This piece of news, blown well out of proportion by an agency report, spread like wildfire and, within hours, became the talk of the country. I was naturally stunned and disturbed. The 'fatwa' that was attached to my name that day and the hastily drawn conclusions by 'knowledgeable' commentators who did not bother to fully comprehend and verify the facts of the matter, confounded me for a long time.

Fatwas are big news, and one pertaining to an international female tennis player was a very big story indeed, particularly at that point of time, when I was all over the media after an extremely successful run at the US Open. I think most people assumed that a fatwa meant an order or edict to kill a person as a punishment for breaking Islamic rules. It was this false perception that was most likely responsible for the controversy snowballing the way it did.

According to the dictionary, 'fatwa' is a legal pronouncement in Islam, made by a religious scholar (called a mufti) on a specific issue based on Islamic doctrines. It's an Arabic word and literally means 'opinion'. Most fatwas take the form of advice on how to be a better Muslim, based on Islamic teachings, in response to specific queries. A fatwa could be on as simple a matter as the right way to eat: with your left or right hand.

It is, of course, possible to rake up a controversy by asking a cleric a leading question and then presenting his 'opinion' in a manner that would provoke a public reaction. If a scholar were to be asked whether he thought my tennis clothing was un-Islamic, I do not see how a conservative, religious man could have answered the question in the negative in the light of the teachings of the religion.

In a similar vein, if a scholar of religion were asked whether it was permissible for a Muslim man to watch a film on television in which a woman dances to music, I am sure he would have to give the verdict that it was un-Islamic. But, again, most importantly, this would not imply that he had issued a fatwa against the lives of all Muslim men who admired a heroine in a film and that he was going to kill them if they went against his edict!

The person who thought it important to raise a question on what he possibly knew was a contentious issue, could have chosen not to highlight the cleric's response in his story. Instead, he went to town with it. Had he bothered to understand the true meaning of the word 'fatwa' and shown the maturity to write with a little bit of sensitivity, I personally believe I would have been spared the burden of living under the stigma of a misunderstood fatwa for a major part of my career.

I have never claimed to be perfect in the way I practise religion and have not tried to justify my actions when I am in the wrong. In today's world, if anybody professes to follow the tenets of their religion to the last word (no matter what faith he or she may belong to), I would like to meet that person. Yet, I have complete faith in all that my religion preaches and stands for in its purest form and this includes the dress code.

The Sunfeast Open WTA tournament was to be held within a fortnight after the cleric had been asked to comment on my attire. Perhaps this had been the intention all along: to capture attention and eyeballs by stirring up controversy on the eve of an international tournament that was being held in the same city (Kolkata). The news channels and other journalists quickly latched on to the story and chose to devote considerable time and space to the perceived threat against me. The discussion around the fatwa appeared to have reached a crescendo.

I was shocked and taken aback to be greeted by a battalion of security personnel when I landed with my mother at the Dum Dum airport in Kolkata on 15 September 2005. The tournament was to begin two days later and several armed men had been deputed to take care of my personal security round-the-clock. The indoor stadium resembled a war zone, with scores of policemen providing a security blanket around me.

I felt suddenly vulnerable and insecure and immediately called my father, who was taking a week off at home after the long American tour. He flew down with Anam within hours and I felt a bit safer, huddled with my whole family in the hotel room.

I was hardly in the ideal state of mind to play after all this and not surprisingly, I had an up-and-down tournament. In the second round, I won the first set at love and then went on to lose the match.

In hindsight, after all the hysteria had died down, the hype did seem exaggerated as there was no specific threat against me although a member of a religious organization was reported to have told a pressman that they would try to convince me to play in more conventionally modest attire. This appeared to be advisory in nature, rather than a serious threat.

Several months after the Kolkata WTA tournament, I happened to watch a television programme in which a member of the religious organization at the heart of the controversy was being questioned by a viewer via a live telephone call. He was asked how he could justify the threat to harm me.

The gentleman categorically replied that Islam did not give him the authority to harm me and that no threat had ever been made. The fatwa merely pertained to what was prescribed according to the teachings of the religion and had nothing to do with harming anybody. He claimed he had tried to clarify several times through press releases that the threat was a misconception and that no such fatwa had been issued by the organization. Unfortunately, his clarification never reached more than a handful of people.

I suppose every person in this world has certain reasons and compulsions for behaving in the way he does. The journalist who developed the fatwa story had his own reasons to break it to the world in the sensational manner that he felt was correct. Any other journalist in his place might have done the same.

Once the question was asked of him regarding my dress, the cleric himself had his own reasons to issue the fatwa that he did in the light of his knowledge about the religion. As a mufti, he must have been compelled to answer the query that was put to him and nobody can deny the truth of his words, going by the teachings of Islam.

As I said, each individual is probably justified in doing what he believes is right in his own sphere but I believe in destiny and the will of God. It was I who publicly and privately paid a very heavy price while so many others got away scot-free. That, I believe, was the will of God and could perhaps be an expiation for my sins. Maybe someday I should seek a fatwa on that!

*

The fatwa had made me a controversial entity in the eyes of a few journalists and it gave them a new handle to get at me. I was still a teenager and learning the ropes of my profession but I realized that it was in my own interests to quickly master the art of skillful diplomacy and tact, and be very careful in everything I did and said.

To be fair, I think Indian journalism too was feeling its way forward in those days. One of the things they were figuring out was how to deal with a female sporting icon, which was a unique phenomenon as far as our country was concerned. The 'newly aggressive Indian media' (as the *New York Times* termed their counterparts in our country) was still trying to find its feet in the wake of the sudden impetus and reach that the electronic medium had provided to journalism.

It was in this atmosphere that I was invited to speak at the prestigious Leadership Summit organized by the *Hindustan Times* in New Delhi. I was asked to share the stage with Miss Universe 2005, Natalie Glebova and Formula 1 race driver, Narain Karthikeyan. Editor Vir Sanghvi was the moderator. I thought the session went off rather well.

I felt relieved as I walked off the stage but soon found myself being whisked away to a room by a friend from the media, along with Narain Karthikeyan and Natalie Glebova. A few journalists stood waiting for us. Natalie, in particular, seemed to be enjoying the focus on herself and answered dozens of questions on a vast spectrum of topics with the confidence befitting a Miss Universe.

Suddenly, out of nowhere, we were asked for our opinion on the views expressed by actress Khushboo on pre-marital sex. She had recently stirred up a massive controversy by saying that Indian men should not expect their wives to be virgins. While Natalie and Narain were rather vociferous in their support for the actress, I on my part, probably due to my inexperience, did not distance myself enough from her comments. I do remember stressing the importance of 'safe sex' though I probably did not specifically clarify that I meant 'marital sex'. Perhaps it was my choice of words that misled some of the journalists. A few suggested in their articles the following day that I had thrown my weight behind Khushboo and endorsed the statements that she had made. Incidentally, I should add that at that point of time, I only vaguely knew what she had said. Most of the coverage about the Summit published the following day was positive, except for the front-page headline in one national newspaper that screamed, 'SANIA SUPPORTS PRE-MARITAL SEX'. It gave me the shock of my life!

My first worry was the disillusionment that my parents and elders of the family would feel on reading the headline. I was glad that at least my mom, who had been present at the Summit, would know exactly what I had said and meant.

The article did not carry much incriminating information but the headline had done enough damage. Social and religious organizations were up in arms and they demonstrated this in no uncertain terms. It angered me no end that a national publication had not thought it necessary to at least cross-check my views before publishing such a sensational front-page headline.

I have never seen my father as angry as he was that day when he spoke to a friend who worked with that same newspaper. 'Your headline is based on your own warped inference, Sania never said that! But even if she erred under pressure from a section of the press, such a question should never have been publicly asked of an Indian teenage tennis player, in the first place. And what was the need to carry this kind of a malicious front-page heading? You work for a responsible publication and should know how sensitive the subject is,' he fumed.

The damage had already been done. It now needed to be controlled.

I immediately sent out a press release, clarifying that I could not possibly have justified pre-marital sex. 'I am deeply pained at the maligning of my image by ridiculous headlines and opportunistic articles written by a couple of journalists to sensationalize a non-issue through misquoting me by using partial quotes, some of which are totally out of context,' I said. 'Attributing a viewpoint that is totally contrary to what I believe in and what I stand for was an attempt to sensationalize a story. It is possible that a poor choice of words on my part led to an absolute misinterpretation of what I meant but such sensitive issues needed to be clarified and confirmed before deriving such false connotations.'

The incident was an eye-opener for me in my constant learning about ways and means to handle the role of a public figure. I was just a teenager who wanted to bring glory to my country and it startled me that every question that I was now expected to respond to on personal, local, national or international matters had the potential to be misinterpreted and consequently blown up.

The editor of the *Hindustan Times*, Vir Sanghvi, came to my rescue with an editorial that sought to set the record straight. This is the gist of what he said:

> *On Wednesday afternoon, Sania Mirza participated in a session at the Hindustan Times Summit in Delhi. Also participating were Narain Karthikeyan, the racing car driver, and Natalie Glebova, the current Miss Universe. I was the moderator.*
>
> *On Friday evening, my jaw dropped as TV channel after TV channel reported that Sania's remarks about the Khushboo controversy at the HT Summit had angered clerics. On Saturday, the newspapers reported this story.*
>
> *The problem was: Sania had said nothing about Khushboo or about pre-marital sex during our session. I should know. I was the moderator.*
>
> *Could it be, I wondered, that some enterprising reporter had grabbed Sania (and Narain and Natalie, who were quoted as agreeing with her) as the session ended, and asked a few leading questions?*
>
> *Possibly. But the reports were quite specific. Sania was supposed to have made these remarks during our session at the HT Summit. Which, I knew, she had not.*
>
> *Perhaps because she feared a repeat of the short-skirt controversy, Sania issued a public statement denying that she had made the remarks attributed to her. Then, she added, for good measure, that, of course, she opposed pre-marital sex.*

The people who burned Sania's pictures had been brought to attend a demonstration and then provided with photos for combusting. There was no spontaneous anger or outrage.

One of the characteristics of the news business – as Sonia Gandhi pointed out, also at the HT Summit – is that we thrive on conflict. We like covering protests. Demonstrations – especially when photos are burned or chappals hurled – make for good pictures. Controversies sell newspapers. And, if they involve stars, they are good for TRPs.

It is not my case that there is anything wrong with this or that we should alter the fundamental character of journalism. But I think that the Indian media have reached the state where we can be easily manipulated by any publicity-hound who offers to generate conflict or to manufacture a controversy.

Phone the TV channels and tell them that fifty people will gather to burn a photo of Sania Mirza – and six camera crews will be there within the hour.

It has now got to the stage where any organization which seeks national prominence has only to target a well-known person or to misuse religion and, suddenly, that organization is all over the media.

But I think that we in the media need also to look inwards. Are we being too easily manipulated?

Is our search for conflict leading to a situation where anybody who behaves in a hostile and unreasonable manner is guaranteed news coverage?

And if Sania Mirza is too scared to mention a fatwa and if she has to issue statements condemning pre-marital sex because somebody objected to remarks she did not make – well then, I think there's something seriously wrong.

*

Dust had barely settled on this issue when I was informed by my agent that I needed to travel to Kochi for a commercial commitment.

The Delhi episode had disturbed me and I was in no frame of mind to face any more hostilities, particularly in a city to which I was a stranger. However, I was told by the organizers that it would be a straightforward session with a few chosen media persons, who had already been informed that only questions pertaining to the product being endorsed would be entertained. I got onto the stage with Malayalam film star Mohanlal, who was also the brand ambassador of the product that I was endorsing.

The very first question that was flung at me referred to the issue of pre-marital sex and I politely requested the media person to stick to queries about the product that was being launched since that was the reason for the press conference. Some of the media men present in Kochi that day were in a belligerent mood and refused to budge. It was a male-dominated crowd, with barely any women journalists.

'What made you go back on the stand of promoting pre-marital sex?' asked one reporter, referring to the headline that had appeared a few days back. 'We are the moral police and you have to tell us what you said earlier about your views on pre-marital sex,' screamed another, as he tried to pressurize me further.

'You are not a pure person, Sania – you have gone back on what you said,' needled another gentleman.

It did not take a genius to assess that some of the people present in the room had made up their minds already about what they wanted to hear from me that day. Controversy was in the air and they were not going to waste the opportunity.

I felt claustrophobic as attempts were made to put words into my mouth which would suit the storyline they had already decided upon. Tennis, or the brand I was there to promote, had no meaning for many of those who had assembled there and the absence of any kind of respect for me or my feelings was evident.

The final straw came when my agents and good friends, Megha Jadhav and Kavita Bhupathi, tried to calm some of the overly-aggressive media personnel down and requested them to stick to questions about the brand as they had been advised earlier. 'We will ask what we want … You stay out of this and shut up' was the rude response they got. Even basic etiquette was thrown out of the window. Some other men joined in the chorus, to raise the ruckus to a dangerous level.

I had had enough! I could not take the kind of disrespect being shown to me or those around me who were just trying to do their job. I was not going to allow myself, my associates or my sport to be humiliated by people who wanted to use me to say things that suited their line of thinking. Even the men sitting on the dais did not say a word in my favour or try in any way to defuse the situation.

All the endorsement money in the world could not stop me that day from taking a stand against such poor behaviour. I got up from the stage and walked out of the media conference.

Of course, this made news. It is not every day that a sportsperson walks out of a press conference as I had done, without bothering to think of the repercussions. But I was a teenager then and did exactly what my heart believed was right. Obviously, it did not go down too well with some of the local scribes. Again, I was branded as being brash and arrogant. Many others did not bother reporting the sequence of events because it would only embarrass them.

The next day, as the news of my walkout spread, I received several congratulatory messages of support from some of the biggest sportspersons and celebrities of my time. While thanking me for upholding the dignity of all athletes, they unanimously complimented me and expressed how happy they were that I had done what they had wanted to do all through their careers but had not found the courage to.

I do not regret walking out that day at all. I would not have reacted like that in a normal situation. I am a reasonable person who does not walk out of a press conference when faced with uncomfortable questions. But I don't like being pushed against the wall and I am certainly not going to allow anyone to break me.

The most important thing I have learnt about fame is that, contrary to what many believe, it does not make life easy. People like to think that everything is available to you on a platter just because you are famous. That may be partially true but everything has a dark side. Obviously, I do not regret being famous nor would I change it for anything in the world. Yes, I miss the fact that I cannot just walk into a coffee shop to sit and chat with my friends. Even when I was eighteen, because of security issues, I could never go for a sleepover to my friend's place. But one learns to deal with such issues. My priorities were clear – I wanted to concentrate on my career and I was willing to give up the few 'normal' things I had to, in order to succeed in a profession that I loved.

18

MY SECOND YEAR ON THE CIRCUIT – 2006

THE SECOND YEAR on the circuit is always a tough one for a tennis player as opponents and their coaches quickly figure out your game and you become a target. If you have done well, you are defending points from the first year and this anxiety adds to the pressure that keeps mounting with every loss. I had achieved a ranking of 31 in my first full year on the senior circuit and maintaining and bettering that standard was never going to be easy.

When a young tennis player breaks through into the highest echelons of the game, she is an unknown commodity and her strengths have an element of surprise. The weaknesses are still to be discovered and analysed and before that happens, the player makes rapid strides and, if she has the talent, quickly climbs the rankings.

By the second year, the rival coaches have watched your game, examined the video footage, and done a thorough analysis of your strengths and weaknesses. The other girls are quickly coached to combat the new kid on the block. That is when the going gets tough and a professional's character, technique, temperament and skills are put to the test.

In the first year, when a player is just beginning to make her mark, there are very few expectations. But these begin to mount once the world has seen you perform creditably. As I mentioned, the pressure of defending points only adds to one's woes and suffering a complete loss of confidence is not a rarity.

In September 2005, when we were at Sunfeast Open in Kolkata, Indian Davis Cup legend Jaidip Mukerjea spoke to Tony Roche on the phone and suggested to me that the former Grand Slam champion would be able to do wonders for my game. He felt that as Tony was an acclaimed master of the volley and a highly respected coach, he would be able to contribute substantially to my tennis. Roche was a living legend and I was excited when Jaidip arranged for a three-week stint with him in Sydney in December 2005. Once he saw me play, he agreed like the others that the dropping elbow was beyond redemption but we still worked hard on improving my serve and volley.

I was very impressed with the way Tony functioned. A strict disciplinarian, he was a coach who believed in adding to a player's natural talents and instincts, rather than making too many changes. He had the experience as well as the expertise and even today, his volleying skills are quite sensational.

After watching me play for a couple of days, Tony felt that I did not have the aptitude to be a great server but I could work towards developing a serve that was efficient and reliable to complement my ferocious groundstrokes. He taught me a new serve and I now started brushing the ball instead of striking it as flat as I used to. The spin made the serve more reliable and as I reached out above my head to brush the ball, it automatically reduced the negative effect of the dropping elbow.

Roche's professionalism is a lesson for all those who want to achieve something in life and his knowledge about the game is revered by his peers as well as the best players of the current generation. He would pick me up on the dot at 9 a.m. every morning from my hotel and we would be on the court till 11.30 a.m. We would start again at three in the afternoon and complete another solid session of two and a half hours. Sophie Ferguson, the Aussie player, was my hitting mate. Tony himself chipped in at times and, as a coach, he did a world of good to my game in those three weeks that I was privileged to spend with him.

Tony Roche was also working with Roger Federer at the time, preparing for the Australian Open. I could hardly believe my luck when one day Tony invited me to his home to meet and hit for a while with Roger on the tennis court in his backyard. I was immediately struck by the simplicity and pleasing manners of the Swiss genius and I found it easy to strike up a rapport with him.

That afternoon, while Mrs Roche prepared tea for us, the great Ken Rosewall walked onto the tennis court in Tony's backyard and I felt absolutely privileged to be where I was, surrounded by greatness. What I also took back of all the three legends on court that day was their plain and easy simplicity.

I was overwhelmed by Roger's relaxed demeanour, which perhaps is the secret of his unbelievable success, apart from his phenomenal talent of course. In the years that I have known him, Roger has grown into arguably the greatest tennis player the world has ever known. However, his modesty surprised me when I first met him and continues to amaze me even today. The achievements and records that stand in his name are numerous and well-known, but that day I discovered what a likeable person he is. He comes across as an unspoilt boy-next-door and fame sits well on his mature head.

My second year on the circuit turned out to be a difficult one. It was not quite catastrophic, but crucial and consistent wins eluded me. I suppose, after the continuous upward climb of my first year on tour, there had to be a downswing. However, I had some significant and memorable victories during the year while going down narrowly in very tight matches to some of the great players of my era.

I beat the highly talented Victoria Azarenka at the Australian Open, Flavia Pennetta in Paris, Meghann Shaughnessy and Katarina Srebotnik in San Diego, Karolina Sprem at the US Open and Aravane Rezai in Kolkata. I then went on to record one of the most significant wins of my career against the legendary Martina Hingis in Seoul for the third top-10 win of my career.

I was handed out some of the toughest draws in the season and ended up playing the world's top players in the early stages. Even in places where I was seeded, I rarely got a decent draw. I lost close matches to Elena Dementieva (thrice), Anastasia Myskina, Jelena Jankovic, Daniela Hantuchova, Francesca Schiavone, Tatiana Golovin, Patty Schnyder, and to Martina Hingis in Dubai, though she beat me easily in Kolkata.

A few days before my singles loss to Elena Dementieva at Wimbledon, I got the sad news of the sudden, untimely death of my first coach, Srikkanth. I had started playing tennis under him as a six-year-old and though I had moved on to other coaches in later years, 'Srikkanth Sir', as I called him, remained my greatest well-wisher and a dear family friend until his death.

An engineer by profession, Srikkanth got into coaching for the love of tennis. In the last few years before his sad demise, he did not look a happy man. Perhaps the world did not treat him the way he deserved to be treated. He appeared to be disillusioned with life. As a family friend and my well-wisher, he was always there for me. He was also Dad's doubles partner in a few State Ranking tournaments and his boyish excitement and cheerful smile after they beat a few local favourites in those tournaments is still a vivid memory.

Srikkanth never meant to cause harm to anybody and perhaps hurt himself more than anyone else with his somewhat erratic way of life, as frustration began to set in. He was prone to depression but tried his best to hide it behind a smiling face. The last time I met him was a few months before his death, when my sponsor, G.V.K. Reddy, honoured all the Indian coaches who had worked with me at a grand reception. That day, as usual, he wished me the very best in life.

His death was shocking. Emotionally, it was tough to deal with – he was after all my 'first' coach and like a younger brother to both my parents. He saw me achieve reasonable success at the international level, as he had always believed I would. I wished he were still alive when I beat Martina Hingis in Seoul later in the season. That would have made him proud.

Having struggled for the major part of the year, I did finish 2006 strongly, reaching the quarter-finals in Forest Hills, Seoul and

Tashkent, and the semi-finals in Kolkata. I had a much better year in doubles than in singles, winning two titles with Liezel Huber on home soil in Bengaluru and Kolkata and finishing as the runners-up in Amelia Island (with Huber), Istanbul (with Alicia Molik) and Cincinnati (with Martha Domachowska).

Despite a reasonable run in the second half of the year, a lot of my critics had already begun to sharpen their daggers and the 2006 Doha Asian Games held at the end of the year gave me just the platform and inspiration I needed to bounce back with a vengeance. In Seoul, four years earlier, I had been a teenager when I won my first Asian Games medal in the mixed doubles. I was now a seasoned professional and felt the weight of responsibility towards my country.

Leander Paes and I converted the bronze from Seoul into a gold medal at Doha in the mixed doubles. I helped India win a silver in the women's team event with Shikha Uberoi and added another silver medal in the women's singles event. I missed the gold by a whisker in the singles, going down in three tough sets to Zheng Jie of China after annihilating the highly rated Li Na 6-1, 6-2 earlier in the tournament. My rich haul added immensely to my confidence.

Despite having dropped in the rankings from the highs of 2005, I had still managed to survive comfortably in the top-100 for the second consecutive year. That, in itself, was an achievement to my mind. I had proven to myself that I belonged at this level and I knew that things would only improve from here.

Former Indian Davis Cupper Asif Ismail worked on tour with me in the summer of 2006. I knew Asif from my junior days, when he travelled with the Maharashtra state players as their official coach. He had since settled in Hong Kong, which was where I met him accidently several years later. I was playing a high-profile exhibition tournament where the likes of the Williams sisters and Kim Clijsters had been invited. It was here that I combined with Kim in the Watsons Water Champions Challenge Cup to defeat Serena and Venus in doubles for the only time in my career. I got along well with Asif during the week and felt that he could help me with his knowledge and experience, particularly on grass – a surface he relished during his playing days.

Asif worked with me during the grass court season and even helped advance my technical skills. However, tennis is a strange game. There are times when you are playing your best and yet wins are hard to come by. You need the rub of the green to go your way. I believe I lacked that in the tournaments that I played in Birmingham, the charming city of 's-Hertogenbosch in the Netherlands, and in Wimbledon that year. But the work that I put in with Tony Roche in December 2005 and then with Asif Ismail in the summer of 2006 contributed greatly to some of the outstanding results that I notched up later in my career.

In a season where not much seemed to be going my way, it was my match against Martina Hingis that completely changed the flow. Sometimes it takes just that one encounter to dramatically alter things. However, it was not the match I won against the Swiss legend but the match that I lost to her a week earlier, and what I learnt from it, that turned things around for me.

19

MEETING MARTINA HINGIS

Martina Hingis will go down in tennis history as one of the celebrated players of my era. She was the face of women's tennis for several years and I remember family friends using her name to taunt my parents while they were nurturing my game in the early days. 'What do you think you are doing? Producing another Martina Hingis?' they would joke.

In January 2002, I came face-to-face with Martina for the first time. I was in Melbourne for the Junior Australian Open. There were demarcated areas for the juniors, who were firmly instructed not to disturb the senior players if they happened to come across any of them. I saw Martina and her doubles partner, the glamorous Anna Kournikova, and gazed at them in awe, absolutely star struck!

It was four years later that I got the opportunity to play against Martina. I lost to her in Dubai and later that year I played her again in Kolkata, in the semi-final of the Sunfeast Open. I believe this is where part of my turnaround started. After struggling for major results, I was in a semi-final and I was feeling confident about my game. The stadium was jam-packed. India's cricket captain, Sourav Ganguly, had come to watch the match as well. I was in pretty good form that week but Hingis overwhelmed me 6-1, 6-0 with some flawless tennis.

The home crowd was naturally disappointed but I was even more dejected by some of the excessively negative comments in the press.

Martina had produced extraordinary tennis, no doubt. She hit the line on dozens of occasions, served brilliantly and succeeded with everything that she tried. But I truly believed that I had not played badly. I came off the court and said, half to myself and half to those around me, 'Did I really play that bad? Because I don't feel like I did.' Ganguly messaged me later saying, 'It's okay. This happens in sport.'

But the mood was quite different in the papers the next morning. 'Sania can never be a match for Martina Hingis' was the general consensus of Indian experts while the less pessimistic writers proclaimed that 'Hingis is in a different class'. I did not agree with them. Martina had played superb tennis on that particular day and I would wait to prove my point when I got another shot at playing against her.

I got that chance less than a week later – in the second round of the Korean Open in Seoul – and I spent a long time discussing the plan with my father before the game, on the phone. He had watched our match in Kolkata and was one of the very few who agreed with me that despite the one-sided score-line, it had been closer than it appeared. We devised our own strategy for the revenge match.

All through the game in Kolkata, Hingis had concentrated on serving very wide on my forehand in the deuce court and wide on the backhand in the ad court. This meant that I was stretched well out of court and found it difficult to attempt a winner while being caught off balance. She followed up the widely angled serve with an immaculate down-the-line to the far corner to dominate proceedings.

In Seoul, I decided to negate her strategy by standing a step further towards the doubles alley and taking away the wide serve from her. When she tried to go wide, I would be in perfect position to return strongly, and with the return of serve being the most potent weapon in my armour, I could dominate the point from there. Of course, I had left the 'T' open and Martina could go down the middle with her serve. But that would have involved a change in her game plan.

While Martina's backhand is impeccable, we had spotted just that little lack of confidence on her forehand side when subjected to intense pressure. I decided I would focus on attacking her comparatively weaker side with the power that I knew I could produce with my forehand.

In Kolkata, I had tended to be a bit passive, not realizing that there was no way a tremendous touch player like Hingis was going to make an error until she was forced to with consistent power play. In Seoul, having learnt from my mistake, we decided I would go for some big shots.

I stayed in the first set with Martina but she broke my serve at a crucial juncture. However, I had begun to get a feel of what I could achieve by executing my carefully devised strategy against her. I stuck to my game-plan and played more aggressively in the second set, which I captured at love. I was in the zone for this part of the match and didn't miss much.

27 September 2006 turned out to be a very special day as I emerged triumphant with a sweet 4-6, 6-0, 6-4 win against the same Martina Hingis who the experts had believed I was incapable of beating. Amazingly, they had made this pronouncement just four days before I beat her. That is how off the mark the media can be sometimes. The morning after my win, suddenly I was as good as Martina Hingis in the eyes of the critics. To me, it felt like the triumph of the sporting spirit, of resilience and self-belief under extreme pressure.

While beating Martina was a personal high, it taught me a lot about the sport itself. That it is such a great leveller, and there is always a tomorrow – provided you work towards it. It's a lesson that has kept me going all these years. One loss is not the end of life or even a career. If you really want another chance, you'll get it. It's just about remaining focused and patient and working hard for it. That has been my attitude in life as well.

Soon after I had beaten Hingis, my phone was inundated with thousands of messages. I remember, most distinctly, the touching message I received from an excited Sourav Ganguly. He had been on the courtside, watching me lose to her in Kolkata, and he was the first to compliment me for turning the tables in such a telling manner, within such a short span of time. 'That is sport for you! Congratulations,' he messaged.

I beat Hingis again, a year later, in Los Angeles. It was the second round of the tournament and this time too, I won in three sets. This was my fourth meeting with her and I had squared the head-to-head score at two wins apiece, after losing the first two matches. That turned out to be the last singles match that I ever played against her.

I remember one particular wristy winner that I played with my forehand on a crucial point. Martina looked perplexed. 'Is that a wrist or what?' she screamed with mock disgust and a wry smile.

Martina Hingis is undoubtedly one of the great champions of her time. I will always look back at my two victories over her in Seoul and Los Angeles with a tremendous sense of pride and satisfaction because she is one of the wiliest players I have ever encountered.

Life can be so unpredictable! In those days, when I was battling against her in singles, I had no idea that Martina and I were destined to script history together on tennis courts the world over. We were also to become fast friends; it's a genuine friendship that I hope will last our lifetimes.

20

THE HOPMAN CUP ADVENTURE

I HAD WATCHED the Hopman Cup on television and was attracted by the format. It is a completely different experience for a tennis player, a mixed team event unlike any other. The super talented tennis stars of the world are invited to compete in the tournament, in which the best male and female players of a country are pitted against those of the other nations. I felt India had the potential to match the best mixed teams of the world and was keen to play the tournament. However, the thought seemed far-fetched at the time as participation was purely by invitation.

The opportunity did come in November 2006 when Paul McNamee, the former World No. 1 doubles player and then tournament director of the Hopman Cup, offered a wild card to one country from Asia that would emerge victorious in the Asian leg of the tournament. The first Asian Hopman Cup was played in my hometown of Hyderabad and the crowds thronged to the stadium as my teammate Rohan Bopanna, who had replaced the injured Leander Paes, and I strung together a series of victories without dropping a set, to win the inaugural edition. We thus earned the right to compete in the World Group of the Hopman Cup to be played in Perth between the eight elite tennis nations of the world.

In those days, the live wire Paul McNamee was the heart and soul of the tournament, which involves stiff world-class competition, intense patriotic rivalry and a whole lot of fun-filled entertainment. The spectators who came for the week were die-hard fans who had been spending the New Year hobnobbing with the latest star players of the Hopman Cup for more than two decades. The matches went out live on television to all of Australia and several other countries. The timing – it being the holiday season, soon after Christmas – made it one of the most watched sporting events Down Under. It provided spectators the ideal start to the year and they kept coming back for more.

As the wild-card entries in the tournament, we were not really expected to give anybody a tough time. We began our campaign against the Czech Republic, represented by the formidable duo of Tomas Berdych and Lucie Safarova. I found myself striking the ball with superb timing on the indoor courts and was delighted to give our team the ideal start with a fluent 6-2, 6-2 win against Lucie in just fifty-five minutes. Though Rohan lost by an identical score-line to Tomas in the men's singles, we notched up an exciting 6-3, 5-7, 10-5 win in the deciding mixed doubles. The victory suddenly made everyone sit up and take notice of the Indian team. The Croatians, led by another top-10 player, Mario Ancic, were up against us next.

I won the women's singles match with another clinical 6-2, 6-2 victory over Mario's sister, Sanja. Rohan played out of his skin and was unlucky to go down in two tough tie-breakers. It came down to the wire in the decisive mixed doubles and Rohan and I maintained our undefeated record together as we won 3-6, 6-3, 10-8 in the super tie-break against the Ancic brother and sister team.

Mario was hugely impressed with Rohan's performance. 'I cannot understand how a player with that powerful serve and a big game cannot break into the top-50 of men's tennis!' he told me at the players' party.

Mahesh Bhupathi had joined us in Perth to train with Rohan and me. He seemed to enjoy the role of 'senior consultant' to our team and was the most vociferous cheerleader in the Indian box. Trainer Heath Matthews and my father made up the rest of our contingent.

The competition at the Hopman Cup was intense but we had a lot of fun together, on and off the court.

The casino on the ground floor of our hotel was a regular haunt for the participating teams and Mahesh, Rohan, Heath, Dad and I decided to check it out, just to get a feel of the place. While the security man at the entrance let the rest of us in, he refused to allow Mahesh into the casino as he claimed that our 'senior consultant' was below the age of eighteen!

Since the boyish looking thirty-two-year-old Hesh did not have any papers to prove his age, we decided to try and get in through another entrance, only to find Mahesh being stopped in his tracks yet again.

'You can go in,' said the six-foot-tall guard in charge of security, pointing towards me. 'But that friend of yours is too young to enter a casino.' We almost choked with laughter.

This was not the only occasion when the usually suave Mahesh was under pressure that week. A leading women's tennis player decided at the players' party that the handsome Indian was the man of her dreams and tried to woo him in no uncertain terms. Hesh managed to give her the slip, but not without a little help from the rest of us in the Indian team.

We had beaten Czech Republic and Croatia and a win against Spain would put us into the final. I started well against Anabel Medina Garrigues, picking up the first set, but the Spaniard, who was to partner me in the upcoming Australian Open that year, struck back to pocket the next couple of sets. Rohan expectedly struggled against Tommy Robredo and though we lost the tie, we did finish undefeated in the mixed doubles as we beat the Spaniards 6-7, 6-2, 10-8. We failed to make the final but made a pretty strong statement for Indian tennis in the mixed event.

*

In the twelve-month period starting with the 2007 Hopman Cup, I probably played some of the best tennis of my career. In many ways, this was a comeback year for me. I had to overcome a serious knee injury, followed by surgery, but despite this I continued to go from strength to strength. If the second year is the hardest on the tour for any tennis player, the third is when you truly come into your own. You have been around long enough, you are respected in the locker rooms, and you know your way around.

The problem for me was the serious injuries that I suffered every time my career seemed to gain momentum. It happened several times that I missed a major chunk of the clay court season with injuries and came back just a week or so before the French Open, which was hardly the ideal preparation for entering a Grand Slam. The year 2007 happened to be one such frustrating year.

I flew down soon after the Hopman Cup to Hobart in Tasmania, where I made a strong start, reaching the semi-final in my WTA season opener. I had morale-boosting wins over Maria Kirilenko, Romina Oprandi and local favourite and former top-10 player Alicia Molik before going down to Anna Chakvetadze.

When I won the Wimbledon girls' doubles title in 2003, Anna had come through the qualifying draw to reach the final in the singles, where she lost after holding championship points. Immediately after Wimbledon, the two of us had played doubles together at the Canadian Open in Repentigny, near Montreal. We had got along well ever since but in this, my comeback year, the Russian proved to be a spoke in the wheel, beating me on four successive occasions. I beat her in doubles, but always found it tough against her in singles. At many crucial points in 2007, she stood in my way.

In the first round of the Australian Open, I sailed past Olga Savchuk and felt confident about my second-round match against Aiko Nakamura, whom I had earlier beaten, but things did not go my way. I practised in perfect, sunny conditions and was happy with the manner in which I was timing the ball. As we entered the court to warm up for the match, it started to rain. We came back after several hours, by which time the weather had changed completely and there was a thick cloud cover.

I just could not time the ball the way I had done earlier in the day and struggled all through a mediocre match. Nakamura beat me in straight sets and I was disappointed with the way I played. A day later, while evaluating the match, Tony Roche gave me some insight into what had happened.

He explained how the ball behaves very differently in cloudy conditions as compared to sunny weather on the courts at Melbourne Park. One needs to adjust one's timing accordingly, he said. When it's cloudy, the ball tends to stick to the surface. It stops for a split second after bouncing and it's not possible to go through with one's strokes. I could only nod in agreement and filed these important notes away in my mind to be used in the future.

I then went on to reach the semi-finals in the WTA tournament in Pattaya and the quarter-finals in Bengaluru. I was unlucky to lose to Yaroslava Shvedova in the Indian tournament, going down in three tough sets in a match that rose to great heights. The Kazakh girl was on the way up and had nothing to lose. She played quite amazingly that week to capture her first WTA title.

In Doha, I was playing against Romina Oprandi for the second time in six weeks when I hurt my right knee. It was a freak injury as my leg stuck to the surface when I tried to change direction and my anterior cruciate ligament (ACL) seemed to be severely strained or torn. Amazingly, I still managed to win that match but had to give a walkover in the next round. When I came off the court after the match, it did not feel so dire. I remember telling Heath, my physio, 'It doesn't feel so bad.' But he insisted we get it checked.

I flew back to Hyderabad the next day and twenty-four hours after that freak injury, I was in surgery. This was a huge setback. The injury had struck just as I had begun to find my rhythm and was nearing my best form. It was a good ten weeks before I could return to the circuit again.

When I look back, I wonder how I managed to be so calm about the surgery. At the time, I was more concerned about how long the recovery would take. I had started to play well and this was a sudden and unexpected dampener to my goals. The doctor gave me two options. One was to wait, take a long break from tennis and check again after three months. Chances were that the knee would become okay on its own. The other option was to get the surgery done right away and go through rehab for two months. This would ensure that I was in perfect shape when I returned. I didn't even blink before telling him I wanted the surgery. I was not going to take the risk of not being able to play after three months.

The only problem was that till I was taken in for surgery, nobody knew if my ACL was partially or fully torn. The difference was mammoth – a fully torn ACL would cost me close to nine months away from competitive tennis. So my biggest worry while being wheeled in was what the surgeons would find. As the procedure started, they asked me to start counting backwards from ten. I was knocked out by the time I got to eight. When I woke up, still heavily drugged, I remember the first thing I asked the doctor: 'So is it nine months or two months?' They said two and I passed out again.

The first time you attempt to walk after recovering from anaesthesia, you feel a massive head rush. I almost fainted in the washroom. Thankfully, my mom saw me in time and held on to me before I crashed to the floor. These are perhaps the more scary aspects of a surgery than the procedure itself. As an athlete, you think of yourself as invincible. You don't think you can get hurt or be sick. But the fact is that you do, and it's not easy dealing with the feeling of being so vulnerable and weak. In fact, athletes are more fragile than normal people because we put our bodies through so much stress and chances of requiring surgery are far greater.

I hated being in a wheelchair and I could not bear the thought of being seen in one. I wanted to walk out of the hospital on my own but the doctors would have none of it. As my mother wheeled me out, a press photographer jumped out from behind a pillar, where he had waited for hours to click me in the wheelchair for the front page of a newspaper, and darted away even as the authorities tried to stop him. He came back a little later without his camera to apologize to me.

'I'm sorry Sania, but I've been under pressure from my employers for this picture. It hurts me, but I had to do it,' he said. 'It's my job and I hope you understand.'

Thankfully, my rehab went well. I was on my feet by the third day but still miles away from being back on the court. I was on heavy doses of painkillers and had lost the use of the muscles in my right leg. Once your body is cut open, there is a severe deterioration in general fitness levels. My physio asked me soon after I came home if I could tighten my quad muscle. I realized I could not because I had no muscle left there. It was the worst feeling in the world. I felt completely handicapped. I had worked so hard as an athlete to build my fitness, and I was perhaps at my physical best at the time when I got injured.

Overall though, things went better than expected. By the second day, I walked up two floors to my room. It was painful but I could do it. It took me twenty minutes, but there was no way I was going to be carried on a chair to my room.

Coming back from a serious injury is always an arduous task but I was happy to record my first singles win at the French Open, beating Alberta Brianti 6-1, 6-1 less than three months post-surgery. This was made possible by my rehab under my physio's watchful eyes. I did fitness training for five hours a day soon after the surgery. We climbed hills with weights tied to my ankles, endured forty twenty-metre sprints and then followed this up with training on stairs. All this, post tennis and a workout in the gym. So, in all, it was almost a ten-hour day for several weeks. But the sweet result of all this work was that I missed only two-and-a-half months of competitive tennis after my surgery.

Clay has never been my favourite surface as the slowness negates the power of my strokes. Not having played on the red clay of Europe during my initial years, my movements are sluggish and lethargic (at least in singles), and make me look like a fish out of water. I had done well in the ITF tournaments on clay but the Grand Slams are a different level altogether.

Spanish coach Gabriel Urpi joined me in 2007 and added another

Sania with her parents at Juhu Beach a few days before their departure to USA in December 1990

Seven-year-old Sania practising on a clay court in Hyderabad, in one of the many tennis attires put together by her mother at home

Dressed as a beggar
for her school's fancy-dress
competition

With her water bottle
during a practice session

With her family and aunt Anjum
(second from left) during one of
her US Open campaigns

Receiving awards at the many State Ranking competitions; (below) in action at one of the tournaments

With the Bhambri sisters, Ankita (second from right) and Sanaa (centre), and their brother Yuki at one of the AITA events in Delhi

Working hard on her forehand in the early days

Acknowledging the cheers of the crowd after winning the WTA singles title in Hyderabad in 2005

Meeting Mary Pierce, winner of two Grand Slams in singles, for the very first time before partnering her at the Hyderabad Open, 2003

With noted tennis coach and Grand Slam winner Tony Roche and trainer Jade Hottes, at their training stint together in December 2005

Lifting the Junior Wimbledon 2003 trophy with Russian partner Alisa Kleybanova

With Mahesh Bhupathi, holding their two Grand Slam trophies won at the Australian Open 2009 (right) and French Open 2012 (above)

With partner Bethanie Mattek-Sands after winning the 2013 Dubai Open title

At the US Open 2005, the year Sania made rapid strides on the professional circuit with breathtaking speed

'Dad's little girl'

Celebrating her Asian Games 2006 medals with her mother at home in Hyderabad

With her parents, sister and Shoaib Malik at her Walima dinner reception in Lahore

Sania and Shoaib at the 'Just Turned One' event to felicitate her on becoming the World No. 1 in women's doubles in April 2015

At the Formula One Indian Grand Prix in 2012

With her parents and younger sister Anam at the Taj Mahal during a visit to Agra in 2015

Under the watchful eye
of her father and coach

The Mirza family at the Great Wall of China
during the Beijing Olympics 2008, with Sania's
doubles partner Sunitha Rao (centre)

With the late Sunil
Dutt, then Sports
Minister, and Congress
President Sonia Gandhi

With the legendary Rod Laver in the Centre
Court named after him at Melbourne Park
just before the Australian Open mixed
doubles final in 2014

At the Sania Mirza Tennis Academy (SMTA), being felicitated by Martina Navratilova (facing page, extreme right) and with trainees at SMTA (below)

With Cara Black and the 6 ft 11" Ivo Karlovic during the 2014 French Open

(Left to right) Scott Davidoff, Shayamal Vallabhjee, Mahesh Bhupathi, Sania and her father after winning the 2009 Australian Open

At the Beijing
Olympics with
Mahesh and 'Scotty'

With Australian cricketers Shane Watson (extreme left)
and Mitchell Johnson (extreme right) and tennis player
Alicia Molik during an exhibition match at Hobart

In celebration mode with Martina Hingis

dimension to my game. The maestro had the experience of working with the likes of former Grand Slam winners Arantxa Sanchez Vicario and Conchita Martinez. He had also been working for a long time with my good friend, Italy's Flavia Pennetta.

Gabi's easygoing nature off-court gives no indication of the thorough taskmaster he is. His extensive knowledge of the game is extraordinary and the circuit is his home. Gabi was himself a proficient player and once took a set from Jimmy Connors at the French Open. He was a specialist on the red clay of Europe and had the best expertise on the surface. Despite being injured, working with him helped me immensely.

I scored a satisfying 6-0, 6-3 victory over Yaroslava Shvedova at Wimbledon in a revenge match after she had beaten me in Bengaluru. My best friend from school, Rucha Naik, had joined me for the grass court season in England and it was fun to have her around. She was graduating with a degree in fashion marketing from the University of Lancaster. Rucha was no sports enthusiast and had very little interest or knowledge of tennis, but she was a friend I loved and cared for. Perhaps that's why she is one of my best friends. I cannot forget the first time she came into the Players' Lounge at Wimbledon. Roger Federer walked up to our table at some point and joked with me.

'What is this guy's name and who does he think he is?' Rucha said rather indignantly as soon as Roger had left the table.

'Oh, he's just a nice guy who hangs around here at tournaments and plays a bit of tennis,' I said, wickedly.

Once, at a time when Jelena Jankovic was ranked No. 1 in the world, Rucha got talking to her at the Players' Cafeteria in Birmingham, entirely unaware of the credentials of the Serbian professional. After spending a good quarter of an hour talking about all kinds of stuff, she asked Jelena, 'What do you do for a living?'

'I am the world's No. 1 tennis player,' replied Jelena Jankovic with her signature laugh, to the utter embarrassment of a hapless Ms Naik.

*

The wins were coming slowly, though surely, but I was still searching for consistency in my singles performance as I headed to USA for the hard court season. It was here that I found the rhythm that had eluded me and I came bouncing back with strong efforts in singles as well as in doubles.

Anna Chakvetadze ended my fine run at Cincinnati in a closely contested three-setter after I had fought my way into the semi-final. Bethanie Mattek and I went on to win the doubles title, which was a fair consolation for the singles loss.

In Stanford, I had a memorable tournament to the delight of the large Indian population there. I started off with a thrilling win in the third set tie-breaker against my old rival, Akiko Morigami, ranked 44 in the world at that point in her career. I then went on to beat Tatiana Golovin and Patty Schnyder – two top-20 players – in straight sets before getting the better of Sybille Bammer, ranked 22. I was having a dream run with four top-50 wins on the trot and it took Anna Chakvetadze once again to spoil my party by beating me in the final. However, I got the better of Anna and her partner Victoria Azarenka in the doubles. Shahar Peer and I won the title with a strong performance.

My good form continued in San Diego as I defeated Peer (ranked 18), Eleni Daniilidou (44) and then added the scalp of No. 14 ranked Russian, Dinara Safina, whom I bamboozled 6-1, 6-2 to assert myself in no uncertain terms on the hard courts of USA. The win over Safina should rank among the high points of my career given that some months later, she went on to establish herself as the No. 1 singles player in the world.

Although I lost the quarter-final to Maria Sharapova, in less than a fortnight I had beaten four top-20 players and another three from the top-50. These were heartening statistics after the despair of the knee surgery just a few months ago.

A straight-set win over Aleksandra Wozniak in Los Angeles paved the way for a match-up again with Martina Hingis and I went on to record my fifth top-20 win of the season. I did end up losing to Virginie

Razzano but maintained my giant-killing run with yet another top-50 victory over Anabel Medina Garrigues (33) in New Haven and Kaia Kanepi (44) at the all-important US Open. I also went on to beat veteran Laura Granville to storm into the third round of the Grand Slam but alas, there stood Anna Chakvetadze again between me and further glory. She stopped my progress for the fourth time that year.

Chakki was at the top of her game in 2007 and was easily playing the best tennis of her life. She reached a career high of No. 6 around this time. She had an unorthodox game and she chipped her stroke at the last moment on both flanks with a subtle turn of her wrist. This made it difficult to read her shots until very late. This unique, natural aspect of her game made her a tricky customer.

Perhaps if I had found the key to beat Anna Chakvetadze that season, I would have risen higher in the rankings, but I still managed to reach a career best of 27 in the world in singles, on 27 August 2007. I sometimes wonder what a numerologist would make of such a remarkable recurrence of the digits 2 and 7!

During the course of this year, I also climbed to a ranking of No. 18 in the world in doubles in September. I had finally had the year I had been working for.

21

DOUBLE THE FUN!

DOUBLES CAME NATURALLY to me, as it does to most Indian tennis players. Even as a greenhorn in international tennis, I won the Junior Wimbledon title in doubles. The brilliance of Mahesh Bhupathi and Leander Paes is testimony to what our countrymen can achieve in this format.

Some of my well-wishers felt that I might have been better off if I had concentrated on doubles rather than singles after the first few years of my career. However, I personally found singles to be far more challenging. Until injury forced me to quit, I could never think of walking away from the opportunity of competing against the best singles players in the world.

There were also those who believed that I could have achieved greater success in singles if I had not put added pressure on my body by playing doubles. I started playing doubles consistently from 2007, while I was still targeting singles success and had broken into the top-30. Perhaps they were right, but I enjoyed playing doubles immensely and the wins gave me both joy and satisfaction. A balance between the two formats was what I was constantly looking for.

I had a particularly successful run in doubles in 2007, winning four titles with as many different partners. After having teamed up and won in Fes, Morocco on clay with Vania King and on the hard courts of Cincinnati with Bethanie Mattek, I went on to capture titles with Shahar Peer in Stanford and with Mara Santangelo in New Haven. I narrowly missed out in Istanbul, finishing as runners-up with Yung-Jan Chan of Taiwan.

I faced many tough contests on the doubles court during this time. A couple of wins in the US hard court season of 2007 still figure very high on my list of memorable matches. The quality of tennis that we brought to those matches was quite sensational. Besides, the level and class of opponents that we faced on both occasions was extraordinary.

Mara Santangelo of Italy and I beat the second-seeded Aussie-Czech team of Rennae Stubbs and Kveta Peschke in the New Haven semi-final and were faced with the daunting prospect of playing the top-seeded pair of Liezel Huber and Cara Black for the title. In my book, Liezel and Cara are perhaps two of the greatest exponents of the women's doubles game and they were combining superbly in those days. Not too many experts gave our scratch Indo-Italian team much of a chance. But in 2007, I was in the middle of one of my best stints in doubles even though I had no regular partner.

Liezel is not only one of my good friends on the tour but was also the partner with whom I won my first three WTA doubles titles in Hyderabad, Kolkata and Bengaluru. We had a tough task ahead of us but that evening, Mara and I annihilated one of the finest doubles teams in the world. We gave them no chance whatsoever, as I found myself hitting the line consistently and the lanky Italian came up with some devastating net-play and overheads. We served well, returned stupendously and volleyed with aplomb. In a totally one-sided match, we destroyed the top seeds 6-1, 6-2. Fittingly, the performance won me the third title of the year's US hard court season and the fourth for the year.

Late that night we travelled in a swanky limousine provided by the tournament organizers to our hotel in Manhattan for the last Grand Slam of the year. It was here at the US Open that Bethanie Mattek and I produced some magic once again to reach our first quarter-final in a Grand Slam. In the third round, we notched up another memorable win – this time against the other world-class team of Lisa Raymond and Samantha Stosur.

I had lost to this pair in two Grand Slams earlier in the year while partnering Eva Birnerova in the French Open and Shahar Peer at Wimbledon. However, Beth and I had a pretty good equation and complemented each other's style of play rather well. We got off to a slow start, with Samantha serving brilliantly and Lisa doing all that a great doubles player of her class and calibre is capable of.

We came back from a set and a break down to edge them 7-5 in the second and then carried on the momentum to win by an identical score in the decider. The match lasted almost three hours as the pendulum swung one way and then the other. At the end of the day, we emerged victorious against yet another top-quality doubles pair. Within a span of ten days, I had got on the winning side against two of the greatest doubles teams of that period and, amazingly, the wins had come with two different partners.

Later in my career came the full shift from singles to doubles, following three surgeries that I underwent within a period of five years. I achieved unprecedented success in the format after reaching a point where I thought I would never play tennis again. Perhaps it was these wins in 2007 that made me believe I could reach the pinnacle in the doubles format, long before it became a conscious goal for me. At the time, I could not have imagined that I would create history by winning six Grand Slams and also becoming the first Indian woman to be ranked No. 1 in the world in doubles. But these two significant wins of 2007, at a time when I was still developing as a tennis player and against a couple of world-class teams, were definitely a forerunner to the way things would pan out for me in doubles and will remain fresh, sweet memories long after I have gone away from the game.

22

THE CHARMINAR CONTROVERSY

In December 2007, Mahesh Bhupathi and I organized a camp in Bengaluru so we could train together during the off-season before we left for Australia. Rohan Bopanna joined us along with Purav Raja, a former national champion. We invited American coach Scott Davidoff and trainer Shayamal Vallabhjee from South Africa to help us in our programme.

Some of the junior kids who had been selected for the Apollo Tyres elite scheme at the Bhupathi Tennis Village chipped in as our hitting partners and together we comprised a serious, hard-working team. We would train and play tennis for about six hours a day, while the evenings were reserved for dinner at one of the fine restaurants in the Garden City. By 10.30 p.m. we were all ready to drop dead!

In the middle of the camp, I flew down to Hyderabad for a day to shoot for an interesting advertisement which would show me as one of the sports achievers of southern India. I was to be projected doing something unique, away from my vocation, while highlighting a prominent landmark of my beautiful city.

As I belonged to Hyderabad, the director planned to shoot me as an artist attempting to paint the Charminar while sitting in front of the famous historical monument. It was not a difficult shot but news of my presence in the Old City, where the Charminar is located, spread like wildfire and a big crowd gathered to get a glimpse of the action. Before we knew it, chaos had descended and the security men struggled to keep the thronging crowds around us under control.

The organizers of the shoot and the policemen who were present advised me to retreat for a while to an area adjoining the Mecca Masjid, which is located directly opposite the Charminar. I was guided into a zone that is not a part of the Masjid. It is a place where visitors or tourists (including women) can click pictures and they are allowed to enter without taking their shoes off. In other words, it does not come under the sanctified part of the mosque and film shootings are allowed in that area, with the requisite permits. We, of course, had no intention of shooting there, we were only looking for a peaceful spot away from the crowd.

As I sat there waiting for the next shot to be readied, a freelance photographer, inconspicuous in the big crowd that stood gazing, took a picture of me with the Mecca Masjid as the backdrop. This photograph then appeared in the local newspaper the next day along with an article that said I had been part of a shoot inside the sacred mosque.

The reporter had shown the photograph to a few influential people in the area and asked for their comments on my alleged 'misuse of the religious monument for commercial purposes'. Needless to say, there were a couple of ill-informed opinions expressed by people who had been deliberately kept in the dark about the actual facts and these were then highlighted in the article. As a consequence, without knowing the truth of the matter, a couple of local organizations decided to flex their muscles.

Funnily enough, the shooting in front of the Charminar had gone off smoothly and I had felt a wonderful rapport with the hundreds of people who had gathered to watch me. I waved to them in response to their loud cheers as I packed up. I was oblivious then, that by the following morning I would be projected as someone who had deliberately hurt the sentiments of my own community.

I flew back to Bengaluru to rejoin the camp the same evening. Meanwhile, that one reporter or rather, mis-reporter, was hatching his plan to project me as a villain. In his over-enthusiasm, he crossed the line and became guilty of professional misdemeanour, in my opinion at least.

For, although the shooting took place in front of the Charminar, he publicly lied that I was misusing the Mecca Masjid for commercial purposes.

I still don't understand why a reporter would even want to instigate public opinion against a sportsperson or any celebrity. Maybe it was to score a few 'brownie' points for himself with his seniors by presenting himself as the only one who had got an 'exclusive' story, ahead of his competitors. I felt hurt and dismayed. And as so often happens when a controversial news item makes its way into one of the publications, the rest of the media felt obliged to carry the story without any due diligence of their own.

I was convinced that I had not done anything wrong and yet had no qualms about apologizing to anyone who felt hurt or let down by me. I immediately wrote a letter of apology and faxed it to my mother, who hand delivered it to the Imam of the Mecca Masjid in Hyderabad that same evening.

This is what I said in the letter:

It is with a deep sense of remorse that I apologize to all my brothers and sisters and respected elders who have been anguished by my unwittingly entering a portion of land belonging to Mecca Masjid while filming the Charminar with the intention of promoting the heritage monument, which is symbolic of our city. While I am fully aware that a woman must not enter the sanctity of the mosque, I was unaware that even entering the outside gates was seriously objectionable, especially without permission, which I was assured by the agency they possessed.

The Imam was extremely gracious while accepting the letter of apology and blessed me and my family. He said that he always prayed for me as he thought of me as his own daughter. His only grouse was that the agency which had organized the shoot had claimed to have the required permits when, in fact, it had not taken permission from the committee for commercial photography.

Though the agency personnel had not actually filmed in the adjoining land belonging to the Masjid, where permission was required for a shoot, they had brought some of their expensive equipment into that area to prevent it from getting damaged by the crowds. That was the reason why the board had felt it necessary to file a police complaint, the Imam explained. Since I happened to be part of the group, my name had also figured in the complaint.

A simple case of unintentional trespass, in which I had unknowingly got embroiled, had been misrepresented by certain vested interests to appear as though I had deliberately tried to demean my own community.

Soon after, in his speech to the Friday prayer congregation, the Imam spoke of how he had received an apology from me and that he was satisfied with the explanation. He said that the matter should now be treated as closed. I do believe that people responded with warmth and I felt as though a huge burden had been lifted from my shoulders. But as has been the case throughout my career, another needless and vindictive controversy was just around the corner.

23

TO THE BRINK AND BACK

ON THE STRENGTH of a fine showing on debut, India received a direct entry the following year into the World Group of the 2008 edition of the Hopman Cup without having to play in the Asian qualifying tournament. This was a huge honour, considering that only the best teams in the world were invited for the event.

We played USA in our first outing and Meghan Shaugnessy pulled off a very tight match against me as I went down 3-6, 6-4, 3-6. Mardy Fish then went on to beat Rohan Bopanna in straight sets but we struck back in the doubles to surprise the solid Fish-Shaughnessy combination 6-4, 6-4 and keep our hopes alive in the tournament.

All eyes were on us as we came up against the home side, Australia, next. I beat Alicia Molik 6-2, 2-6, 6-4 in a match that had the partisan home crowd screaming for blood. The encounter lasted an hour and fifty minutes and kept the spectators on tenterhooks all through. Peter Luczak brought parity with a straight-set victory over Rohan and that set the scene for yet another pulsating mixed doubles decider.

We split the first couple of sets and held our nerve in the super tie-break, winning at 13-11 and sending shock waves amongst the home team's fans. The packed house was stunned. We had not only denied the host team a spot in the final but also knocked them out of contention. And we were still in with a chance of making it to the final, depending on how the other teams in our group fared in their last match.

My three-set loss to Lucie Safarova in our tie against the Czech Republic proved costly for us as Rohan was always going to struggle against Tomas Berdych. However, quite remarkably, we continued with our unbeaten run in the doubles, beating the Czech duo easily in straight sets. Rohan and I had now won nine consecutive mixed doubles matches in the two years that we had participated in the Hopman Cup. In the process, we had outclassed some of the world's best combinations. A few years earlier, we had won the national title as well, winning four matches in a row, which meant our career record read 13-0 as a combination.

India finished at a commendable third spot in the World Group of the Hopman Cup in 2008 for the second consecutive year. However, a needless controversy reared its ugly head soon after the end of the tournament. This one really shook me and it took a long time to mentally recover from this unwarranted attack.

While I was boarding the flight to Hobart to play in the WTA World Ranking tournament, which is a run-up to the Australian Open, I got a call from my mother. She sounded extremely upset. A photographer had managed to take a picture of me sitting in the players' box while I was cheering for Rohan in his singles match in Perth. Only, it was clicked from an angle that gave the impression that my feet were touching the Indian flag. In truth, the 6" x 9" paper flag was at a completely different angle and was several feet away from any part of my body. It wasn't even placed in the direction in which my feet were pointed. However, once again, without checking or corroborating facts, the media decided it was fine to milk the story.

On the basis of this false image, a gentleman went to court and filed a case against me, alleging disrespect to the Indian flag. This was additional fuel for the TRP hungry media. And it hurt me where it hurts the most – the heart. Coming as it did, after a string of other cooked-up controversies, it left me very disillusioned with life. This was the lowest moment for me in my relationship with the media. Until then, the controversies had been hurtful but I had felt I could ignore them and carry on.

But this was the most ridiculous charge that had ever been concocted against me. I had never imagined I would be accused of disrespecting my own country. Representing India was the ultimate honour for me and I had worked incredibly hard for it. Being called 'unpatriotic' was more than I could handle.

I had just finished a match that went on for over three hours. I was sitting and watching my partner in action, preparing myself mentally to play the mixed doubles. I was playing for my country, with 'India' written on my back. I was tired and cramping up. So I put my feet up and all this lensman could think of was how to get eyeballs for his paper by being clever? I was too disheartened to even bother to explain to anybody what had happened.

As the Australian Open drew near, I was in a state of depression. I thought to myself, 'This is getting too much. What is all this for? I am twenty-one years old. I can go start another life. Why do I need to go through this? I am patriotic. I have given my blood, sweat and tears to play for the country. Why do I have to justify myself to people? Why do I need to tell them I love my country over and over again?'

I sat down with close friend Mahesh Bhupathi and my father before the Australian Open and told them I wanted to retire after the tournament. They were shocked. 'What the hell are you talking about?' Mahesh said. 'I can't do this anymore, Mahesh. I can't deal with these people anymore,' I wailed.

'You must be joking! You can't throw away everything you have worked for because of a few stupid people!' Mahesh said, almost pleading with me. 'But what am I doing this for?' I replied, sobbing. 'We are playing tennis for our country. And I am being accused of insulting her?'

As an athlete, you have this innate desire to represent your country. You cannot help it. It's almost like being a soldier. Our jobs are nowhere as dangerous, difficult or life threatening as theirs, but playing for the country is the one small way in which we contribute to our nation. It enriches the entire experience of being a sportsperson.

I was still very distraught and cried every day. I was going into the first Slam of the year, hoping to beat the best in the world, while back home I was being labelled a 'traitor'. It was insane!

When the case was filed against me for alleged disrespect to the Indian flag, Roger Federer was among the first to enquire about the situation and my welfare when I reached Melbourne for the Australian Open. He also surprised me many months later with a message of concern when Mumbai was tragically struck by terrorist attacks on 26 November 2008. I think this is what makes Roger very, very special because apart from being a legend, a genius and the greatest ever exponent of his craft, he remains warm, caring, accessible, untouched by fame, and a thorough gentleman.

Back in Australia, Mahesh, my family and friends did their best to dissuade me from my decision to retire. Every now and then, Mahesh or his sister Kavita would e-mail me a positive article that they had come across, to cheer me up. One such piece was written by a journalist, Sanjay Jha, on the eve of the Australian Open. It was titled: 'Sania, Bhajji and Mera Bharat Mahaan'. At the time, cricketer Harbhajan Singh too was facing a raging controversy during India's tour Down Under. Jha wrote:

> *I also see the rising dark face of pseudo Indian nationalism. Why aren't we Indians taking to the streets against an extremely malicious campaign alleging an insult to the Indian tri-colour, the national flag against Indian tennis sensation Sania Mirza? Here is a young, hard-working girl from Hyderabad who has single-handedly battled several odds to achieve a global distinction for her ferocious forehands and relentless power-hitting in a popular sport, hugely competitive and highly demanding. The fact that she is a Muslim, a woman, and an Indian succeeding in a hard-fought tough world where she has not had the advantage of an existing system for grooming talent, of Nick Bollettieri-kind training, fat sponsors, full-time travelling coaches, fitness instructors, easily available infrastructure – should make all of us proud of Sania Mirza.*
>
> *Mirza is a fairy-tale story of individual determination,*

of being innately gritty, of fighting hard against several insurmountable barriers and achieving great success. She is only twenty-one. And has an exciting future ahead. She needs our support. She needs India's support, just as Harbhajan did. She needs the same emotional resonance from us that echoed when Bhajji was summarily damned. The only difference is that in Sania's case, tragically enough, the obdurate opposition is coming from within.

She has been mercilessly hauled up for wearing skirts, maligned for looking glamorous, and been made into a gossip feature at the slightest provocation, even if making a fleeting appearance in a party. Is it her fault that she is a lovely young woman who plays her sport with passion, and has now become a charming celebrity at a young age of twenty-one? We ogle Maria Sharapova and endorse her commercial deals, deifying her like a diva, but Mirza' every move is condescendingly criticized and mockingly rebuked. If she loses early in a Tier 4 tournament, we blame it on her party-hopping and photo-ops. The next day when she beats a Patty Schnyder or a Martina Hingis, we say it was only a rare fluke.

Why aren't we running petition campaigns for Sania Mirza on our TV channels? Where is the collective Indian outrage outpouring in her support? Why are we not worried about the grievous harm all the trumped up accusations can do to a vulnerable young woman in the international spotlight just prior to the year's first Grand Slam starting within a few days? Are we even aware that despite injuries she was fighting hard for India, for her country in the Hopman Cup? Didn't she help bring India several medals at the Asian Games in Doha?

Harbhajan Singh has at least several teammates, an obsessed nation of cricket-crazy followers, a powerful institution like the BCCI and universal media support to espouse his cause. For Sania Mirza, the battle is a lot lonelier. The double-fault is her own personal anguish, as is the easy missed volley. For her, Team

India means every Indian who believes in her. Has faith in her actions. Who does not cheer her shots hit into the bottom of the net. And sees in her success the victory of India.

Mahesh Bhupathi, India's tennis player and a role model for many, has publicly stated that Sania has been shattered by the unending deluge of recent assaults on her. It can, frankly, break anyone. It is human. And this just when she had refused a lucrative commercial contract to represent her country when she has been seeded at the Australian Open.

Did the media and the rest of us Indians even discuss the fact that the reputed Tennis *magazine has rated her deadly forehand amongst the top three forehands of all time? In a few days Bhajji will be in Perth for the next Test match. On Monday, January 14th Sania Mirza will play in the first round against Iroda Tulyaganova of Uzbekistan at Melbourne. By a strange coincidence they will both be in Australia.*

The scoreboard will read: SANIA MIRZA – INDIA.

India, a country of a billion people, and counting. Should we feel proud as Indians if we let that young girl out in the middle feel lonely and lost?

Tears filled my eyes as I read this moving, emotionally charged article. I cried uncontrollably, like a child, and shut myself up in a room for several hours, refusing to come out. But the anguish gradually gave way to determination, resilience and the will to fight back. I once again began to believe that I owed it to myself and to my country to live the dreams of millions. A few stray individuals were not going to spoil our party.

I beat Iroda Tulyaganova a few days later in the first round and followed it up with a win over Timea Bacsinszky of Switzerland before losing in a tight match to Venus Williams in the Rod Laver Arena. The two victories in singles helped improve my world ranking and pushed me ahead of Li Na of China, making me the highest ranked Asian woman in world tennis. It was also the first time that an Indian had reached the top spot in the continent.

This first Grand Slam of the year 2008 was almost like the start of a new era for me. I enjoyed my best Australian Open, reaching the third round in singles, the pre-quarter-final in doubles and also, most importantly, was the runner-up with Mahesh in the mixed doubles. It was the first Grand Slam final for any Indian woman, and came at a time when I was not only managing a serious injury but was also deeply unhappy. I believe my on-court performances raised the level of Indian tennis further and also increased my own hunger to achieve excellence and to win a Grand Slam.

Sports columnist Rohit Brijnath put things in perspective in his article in the *Hindu* a few weeks later and I was grateful for his understanding.

> *A girl sweats. Cramps. Sits. Puts up tired feet that have been running for India. A flag is close by, as flags often are at sports events, and this one is Indian.*
>
> *A photographer takes a picture seemingly from a clever angle that juxtaposes feet and flag. A case is filed in court. Someone, dutifully, alerts the media. And this non-issue becomes a story. Welcome to Sania Mirza's world.*
>
> *As this story crosses oceans, and questions come like a storm, and that sly picture winks from front pages, it's worth wondering: what sort of mental state did Sania take into the Australian Open? How do you function as an athlete when you're accused of disrespecting a flag you play for? Is it possible that tennis can be fun when the discussion about you concerns not serves but short skirts, not lobs but leg showing, not footspeed but flag kicking?*
>
> *That Sania has managed to get to No. 27 in the midst of all this seems pretty good, wouldn't you think?*

*

Despite having had a successful trip Down Under in terms of results, this was not the time to celebrate as off-field controversies continued to consume my time and mental space. I began my preparations to fight the legal case that had been filed against me. We appointed lawyers and with the help of Paul McNamee, I acquired the recording of the match in which I was alleged to have put my foot on the national flag. The footage clearly showed that nothing of the sort had happened and that my feet were nowhere close to the flag.

A few months later, the case of 'disrespect to the Indian flag' filed against me was dismissed by the judge on a technical point. I found it disappointing that very few newspapers reported the dismissal of the case and those who did, thought the news to be fit only for a small column in the back pages. The filing of the case against me was front-page news but the dismissal of that case was not even considered worth reporting by many.

There was one major fall-out of the flag controversy and it still rankles. Despite finishing third for the second year in a row, the organizers of the Hopman Cup, perhaps disturbed by finding themselves in the midst of an unnecessary controversy, decided to omit India from their list of elite nations. We were not invited to Perth the following year.

24

BANGKOK TO BENGALURU

I WAS NOT in the best frame of mind on 28 January 2008 as I boarded the flight for Bangkok where India was to play in the Asia/Oceania Zone Group I of the Fed Cup. The tear in my adductor muscle that had troubled me during the later stages of the Australian Open was extremely painful and after the exertions of the Grand Slam final, it stung even when I walked – or rather limped.

Playing in the Fed Cup has always been very special to me. Tennis can be a lonely sport and whenever one is part of a team, the camaraderie adds to the excitement. I have been privileged to be a part of the Indian contingent since my debut in 2003, when I won my first three matches on the trot. Since then, I have played regularly except in the years when serious injuries kept me out.

My greatest ambition was to carry India into the World Group of the Fed Cup but after having tried my best for years, I now realize that the only way to make that happen is for us to have a bunch of at least three, or preferably four, top-100 players on the team. In a team championship with a physically demanding format, just one player in the top-50 is not going to get us into the World Group.

In the Asia-Oceania Group that India figures in, we need to beat at least four countries in less than a week in best-of-three ties. The team that has generally emerged victorious and gone through to the play-off for the World Group is the one with a handful of top-100 professionals as it gives them the liberty to rotate different players and fresh legs make a big difference. As the only top-50 level player on our side, I had to face the Herculean challenge of attempting to win all eight matches (four singles and four doubles) over five or six days in order to ensure our passage into the World Group and I ran out of gas on many occasions in the decade when I played in both formats.

There have been a couple of times when we did come very close to entering the World Group. Ankita Bhambri gave me able support in 2006 in New Delhi and then Shikha Uberoi and I all but saw us through to the elite group in 2007 in Korea.

I have often injured myself trying to push my body to the limits in the week of the Fed Cup and had to skip the next few World Ranking tournaments on the circuit. In 2008, I put my body on the line yet again.

Upon joining the team, I explained to Enrico Piperno, the Indian Fed Cup captain, that although I wanted to be courtside with my teammates, Sunitha Rao, Shikha Uberoi and Isha Lakhani, there was no way I could be of much use to the team apart from giving a morale boost to the girls. The injury was a big blow to Indian aspirations and Rico was obviously as disappointed as I was.

My physical trainer and the doctor who had examined me in Melbourne after the mixed doubles final were unanimous in their prognosis. The 6 cm tear in my adductor muscle could become career threatening if I played now.

I screamed myself hoarse on the first three days, trying to urge my teammates on, but the writing was on the wall. India lost to New Zealand, Australia and Indonesia and the team was now staring at the humiliating prospect of being relegated to the Asia/Oceania Zone Group II. It had been a few years since we graduated out of that group and we had even come close to qualifying for the World Group in the last two years. Another loss could undo the hard work that gave us the highs of 2006 and 2007.

We were now in the unenviable position of having to play Hong Kong in the relegation play-off. The girls were nervous and the skipper was edgy. He looked towards me on the eve of the Hong Kong tie.

I pressed my fingers against my torn muscle, which still hurt when I moved, as though there was a knife lodged in my upper leg. All I could do was shake my head in despair.

I took a short walk away from the others and stood alone for a while as all kinds of thoughts filled my head. The circumstances were unique and called for desperate measures. The time for rationality was long past. I felt a sudden rush of blood and the desire to do what I could to help India win, even at the risk of further injury.

The doctor and trainer would have none of it and I knew they would not give me the green signal for self-destruction. My trainer had made it quite clear to me that if I played, I ran the risk of hurting my back. But I walked up to Rico and said, 'I don't think I can win a singles match on one leg, skipper. But if one of our girls can win a match for us, I'm ready to play a live doubles rubber.'

Shikha won the first singles for us, beating the tall, lanky Jessica Yang, but Zhang Ling equalized for Hong Kong with a straight-set victory over Isha Lakhani. With defeat staring us in the face, I got up from my cheering seat to warm up for the critical, all-important doubles, which would now be the decider. The trainer looked aghast. 'You are not serious!'

I had a dose of painkillers that partially numbed me for a while but also made me feel nauseous. I knew I could not survive for long on the court and needed to defeat the talented Hong Kong duo of Zhang Ling and Jessica Yang before the pain became unbearable.

In a charged and tense atmosphere, with me playing as though for my life, Sunitha and I won the deciding doubles 7-6, 6-2. There were sighs of relief in our camp. Rico was a happy man that evening. But I almost collapsed at the end of the match. With the effect of the multiple painkillers wearing off, I could not sleep and somehow got through one of the most uncomfortable nights of my life.

I limped along for the next few weeks and was even bed-ridden for three days due to intense pain in my torn leg muscle. I had to skip the next few events on the calendar and to add to my woes, my trainer's prediction came true. I woke up late at home the day I returned from

Bangkok and realized I had a slip disc. I had compensated for the lack of leg movement with extra pressure on the back.

When I did play my next two tournaments in Doha and Dubai, the results were expectedly below par, although I beat the 44-ranked Vera Dushevina in the first round in Dubai for my only win in two events. My wrist had now grown extremely painful and the adductor muscle tear that I had suffered during the Australian Open had still not healed completely as a result of continued exertion.

I was beginning to feel emotionally drained, battle-scarred and bruised. The two recent controversies within a span of one month had taken a big toll on me and left me mentally jaded and fatigued. And these were not the only controversies that were raked up during this period.

The orthopaedic surgeon who had operated on my knee with great skill happened to casually mention to a friend that he had received an anonymous letter from some kind of a maniac. The writer advised him to refrain from treating my knee injury as it was God's way of ensuring that Sania Mirza would not play tennis anymore!

The friend probably repeated the story to another and this 'vital' piece of information reached a reporter almost eight months after I had recovered from surgery. Despite the passage of time, the reporter considered it newsworthy, fit for the front page.

Any well-known person will vouch for the fact that in every bag of fan-mail that reaches him or her, there are at least a couple of letters that make no sense whatsoever. They are written by individuals who are delusional, probably not normal or, at best, eccentric. With experience, one learns to ignore these and not make much of them.

But this particular piece of information was blown up by the reporter to sound as though an entire community (which happened to be my own!) had launched a war against me. Strangely, such petty stories often make their way across oceans and continents. I got a worried call from my aunt, who lives in the US, and she sounded paranoid. 'Treat Sania and Annoy Allah' was the headline of the 'sensational' story on a news channel in her part of the world!

At a time when I needed to concentrate on my game, I was constantly hounded by questions about inconsequential events. The frequency with which these non-issues were raked up and made to sound contentious was a dampener for me, and in my opinion, for my country as well.

Of all the controversies, the Masjid and flag issues had scarred me badly and I didn't think I could handle another such episode at this stage of my career. If the past was anything to go by, the chances of another controversy erupting while I was playing in a tournament in India were sky high. Even the storm around the flag was clearly a spillover from the six-week period I had spent in India, when controversies were being manufactured on an almost weekly basis.

Mahesh Bhupathi had stood by me like the proverbial Rock of Gibraltar through these enormously tough times. He knew how much I had suffered and had seen me go through hell in the last two months. We both felt that, in the circumstances, it might be a good idea for me to take a break and skip the upcoming WTA tournament in Bengaluru. I felt I needed to recuperate physically and emotionally and my family was with me in this decision.

I have always believed in calling a spade a spade and I didn't beat around the bush when I announced that I would skip the Bengaluru WTA tournament because of the pressures I felt due to the recent spate of controversies. Most of the sports journalists were sympathetic and appeared to agree with me even though there were a few who tried to find some ulterior motive behind my move.

But the whole battle was being fought in the media now and things quickly went from the logical to the hysterical. What was shocking for me was the attitude of some of the 'stalwarts' from the tennis fraternity, from whom I had expected understanding, if not unconditional support, as far as my decision not to play in Bengaluru was concerned. There were suggestions that the tournament was being held to benefit players like me and it wasn't right that I should give it a miss. Eventually, they even went on to take the line that they 'didn't need Sania'.

While playing in any tournament is a player's privilege, the Bangalore Open was not organized solely for my benefit and to project it as a favour to me was preposterous. Secondly, to make it an ego battle against one of our own was taking it too far when I had clearly spelt out my reasons for skipping the tournament. A little perspective would have done us all some good.

Each one of these players or ex-players was close enough to me to have been able to pick up the telephone and enquire about my well-being, at the very least. Instead, they preferred to go to the media with ridiculous statements. When the controversy reached boiling point, Larry Scott, chief executive of the WTA at the time, arranged a special conference call for me with someone called Ari Fleischer. I later found out that he was earlier White House press secretary for former US President George W. Bush.

Both Scott and Fleischer, who was now advising the WTA as well, had witnessed the controversy raging around the Bangalore Open and wanted to speak to me on how to manage the media. So here I was, getting tips from the man who once handled a US Presidential campaign and later became the President's first press secretary!

While I listened to their views, I also told Fleischer he needed to come to India once in order to have a better idea of just what I was dealing with. All I had said was that I did not want to play one tournament, over one week, in India and somehow that was construed to mean I never wanted to play in or for India again!

'But that is not fair,' he admitted, sounding a bit confused.

'Exactly,' I said. We had a good chat but India never hosted a top women's WTA tour event again.

Thankfully, strong backing for me and my decision not to play in the Bengaluru WTA tournament came from the biggest names in Indian journalism. Some of them called me personally to convey their support, mailed me inspiring pieces that lifted my sagging spirits and then publicly defended me on forums in the electronic media. I remain grateful to them for standing by me at that critical juncture in my life.

Rohit Brijnath once again sprang to my defence, subtly describing it as 'unfortunate that in India's small tennis fraternity, older men who have no idea what it means to be seen as young, female, gifted, glamorous, a top-30 player and role model, felt the need to criticize Sania's decision to skip the Bangalore tournament.'

Amongst a host of other moving articles, the one I have preserved for inspiration was written by Barkha Dutt of NDTV, a woman whom I have admired for her guts and dynamic personality. It is hard not to agree as she analyses the reasons that made my life difficult:

What if Sania Mirza had been a man? Would she still have been at the epicentre of a strange and stormy love-hate relationship with her country? Would she still have evoked reactions that tend to swing between extremes of adulation and annoyance?

Could it be that the cascading hair, the gleaming nose ring, the cheeky I-don't-give-a-damn T-shirts, the indisputable confidence that often borders on brashness is exactly what makes some people so uncomfortable? When Sania says she feels hurt or fed up at constantly grabbing the headlines for the wrong reasons, it's an understandable reaction.

In India though, while we have watched (in breathless awe and bewildered fright) women storm successfully into several all-male zones, the breakthrough has hardly been that dramatic when it comes to the rough and tumble of the sporting world. If you think I'm wrong, name me an Indian sportswoman (other than Sania) who has a national following or is even recognized or written about regularly.

She's quite simply the only female sports icon India has ever known. And our contradictory responses to her say something about how we respond to women who are non-conformist trailblazers and not afraid to be themselves. It's almost as if we admire them and resent them at the same time.

We can barely deal with men who set their own rules; to ask us to accept a woman who is individualistic, passionate, beautiful and yes, possibly annoyingly arrogant, makes us just a little nervous. There's no doubt that many of the controversies that have tailed Sania have been ridiculous, unfair and often downright inane. From the length of her skirt to her religious beliefs; from fundamentalist fatwas to hyper-patriotic expectations, Sania has had to live in the gaze and battle unprecedented and relentless scrutiny.

India may have been unfair to Sania Mirza, but she can't let herself down. Not now – when she's already changed the rules of the game.

25

OLYMPIC DREAMS

I WAS INCREASINGLY popping pills to manage the pain in my wrist and other parts of the body as well. In Indian Wells in March, playing against Shahar Peer, I was facing another stiff contest. It turned out to be a marathon of a match which I won 7-5 in the third set on an extremely windy day. My wrist was in bad shape and the conditions made it worse. That's when I should have stopped and heeded the warning signs but it was unimaginable at the time to take a break right after a good win. I swallowed more painkillers and even played a doubles match soon after.

I am not sure what I was thinking then, but I continued to play on, going into my third-round singles match against Daniella Hantuchova. I was in uncontrollable pain by then. I lost the match and was relieved to be off the court.

I started working out on the bike afterwards to cool down, as part of the normal routine to get the lactic acid out of my body. But when I tried to press a button, I just could not. It was cold and my wrist was extremely sore. The adrenaline had helped me finish the match, but I knew my wrist had snapped. I had pushed it to the limit and it had finally come undone.

I had just started working with Dutch coach Sven Groeneveld. He had expressed interest in coaching me some years back but at that time, I had already hired the services of John Farrington. It's unfortunate that I suffered a serious wrist injury in my first tournament with Sven. Over the next few months though, he continued working with me.

I immediately consulted a doctor in Mumbai, who suggested I get a surgery done in the US since they had little experience in India of a complicated procedure of the wrist. So I rushed to Miami to meet a specialist. Ten days later I underwent a wrist surgery.

The wrist is perhaps one of the most sensitive and difficult parts of the body to be operated on. The bones are small and intricately connected. A small error by the surgeon can adversely affect the movements of the hand permanently.

I was told that rehab after the surgery could take up to a year but I did manage a return to the courts in six weeks. At the time, I was wrongly advised to continue playing through the pain when a six-month break and rehab would have been the better choice. But the clock was ticking for the Olympics and I constantly felt the pressure to return to the courts as soon as it was humanly possible to do so. The surgery itself was uneventful but the rehab this time was torturous. I had a different trainer and maybe I didn't get the best advice. Together, these made a very bad situation worse as I rushed my return, risking permanent damage to my wrist.

At Wimbledon, I lost to a qualifier in the second round, after having had a clutch of match points. The power of my ground strokes seemed to be missing and I felt severely handicapped while combating world-class opponents. The situation was no better by the time the Olympics came by and I was slipping into depression. The mental pressure had grown to such a point that I broke down before leaving for the airport to catch a flight to Beijing. I was sobbing when I told my father, 'There's too much pain. I can't play.'

My dad, perhaps unaware of how bad the situation was and knowing the importance of playing at the Olympics, convinced me to go. Deep down in my heart, I was desperate to play and needed only that slight push from him. There was a resolve somewhere within me but I was stuck between the painful wrist and reality.

*

A life without dreams is not worth living. And if a few of those dreams come true, they give you the greatest high you can ever experience.

When I set out to become a tennis player ages ago, I always dreamt of playing at the Centre Court at Wimbledon and I was lucky to fulfil my ambition. Somewhere along the way, the dream of representing my country at the Olympics began to take shape and gradually, the dream turned into an obsession. After my wrist injury in March 2008, I had just one goal in mind – to recover in time to represent my country at the Beijing Olympics that were scheduled for August that year.

In the last decade or so, most tennis players have realized how important it is for them to mark their presence at the Olympics. The unique opportunity of representing one's country on the biggest sporting platform in the world motivates them to give their best. However, when tennis first became an Olympic sport, many of the senior tennis professionals stayed away from it. Initially there were no ranking points to be won either – they were added later to make it more lucrative for the professionals.

When I entered the Beijing Olympic Village in 2008 for the first time, I almost had to pinch myself to believe that it was for real: I was here and I was the first woman to represent my country in women's singles in Olympic history.

However, I now know that one cannot argue with destiny. While I was playing my singles match against Iveta Benesova of Czechoslovakia, the pain in my wrist became unbearable as even the potent tablets that I had ingested stopped working. I was forced to throw in the towel and ended up crying uncontrollably on the court. My opponent came to pacify me and only succeeded in losing her own cool. Seeing my discomfort, she inexplicably started to cry as well. Somehow, emotions tend to run high at the Olympics!

I still went into my doubles second-round match. Sunitha Rao and I fought doggedly against the formidable Russian pair of Svetlana Kuznetsova and Dinara Safina but fell short, although we did have our chances in both the sets against the top seeds. The painkillers that I had downed allowed me to compete for a while but after the match, I felt very sore and numb up to my forearm.

I remember thinking to myself that day, how fortunate we tennis players are. There are four Grand Slams to compete in every year, which allows us to perform on the world stage in view of millions of people once every few months. The Olympics gives us that one additional opportunity. But for a lot of other sports, the Olympic Games provide the one and only platform to achieve greatness. It takes a lot of effort to be able to prepare and then time yourself perfectly for the quadrennial event.

My thoughts were with my colleagues, Mahesh Bhupathi and Leander Paes, who had made it to the quarter-finals. However, they were outplayed by none other than Roger Federer and his talented partner Stanislas Wawrinka. I was emotionally charged as I watched the match, trying to live my own dream through the success of the boys, but it was not to be. Mahesh and Leander will probably be remembered as one of the great doubles teams in history not to have won a medal at the Olympics. Similarly, the greatest singles player of our time, Roger Federer, has not yet won a gold medal in the event he excels in. But, as I said, you cannot argue with destiny.

The experience of the Olympics extends far beyond the realms of victory and defeat. There are so many memories to treasure for a lifetime. Interacting with sportspersons from all over the world was an invigorating experience for me. There is an instantaneous connection and bond one feels with fellow athletes, irrespective of language or culture. This is the spirit of the Olympics, the spirit of humanity, and this is what we all probably take back in fair measure from the biggest sporting show on earth.

26

MY FIRST GRAND SLAM TITLE

WHEN I LANDED in Melbourne in January 2009 to play in the Australian Open, I was in a pensive mood. Mahesh and I had lost the final of the mixed doubles the previous year and that had been very disappointing. Considering that it had been my first ever Grand Slam final, the loss could have been crippling if I did not have the support of an amazing team that helped me overcome the blow. I was also recharged with the burning desire to own a Grand Slam title.

The loss in the 2008 Australian Open final to Serbia's Nenad Zimonjic and China's Tiantian Sun still hurt after all these months. In the semi-final, I had torn my adductor muscle and struggled with my movements and yet the final was a fiercely fought match that could have easily gone our way. I had wanted a Grand Slam so badly but the chance seemed to have slipped away. 'Will I finish my tennis career without a Grand Slam title against my name?' I had wondered then and the same disturbing thought crossed my mind as I checked into the Melbourne Hotel exactly a year after the loss.

A lot had changed in the past twelve months. I was on yet another comeback trail, having had surgery on my right wrist, and my rankings had plummeted following my absence from the circuit for almost the entire second half of the year. I barely got into the main draw of the singles but there was very little chance of playing in the mixed doubles, where the cut-offs are extremely high.

Mahesh was adamant, though, that he would only play with me – even at the risk of missing out. We requested a wild-card entry on the basis of our runners-up finish the previous year and thankfully, the tournament committee gave us the spot. Together we played magnificent tennis that fortnight. Starting with a 6-2, 6-4 win over Kveta Peschke and my ex-partner, Pavel Vizner, we went on to outplay Anastasia Rodionova and another ex-partner, Stephen Huss. We played our toughest match in the quarter-final against the Canadian team of Daniel Nestor and Aleksandra Wozniak. After losing the first set, we were in danger of being knocked out of the tournament when, magically, both Mahesh and I struck a purple patch to emerge victorious via the super tie-break after winning the second set.

Once again, though, it felt as if the universe was conspiring to stop me from giving my best in a Grand Slam event, which is the true test of a tennis player's class and calibre. I injured my stomach muscle just under my rib during the quarter-final and the scan showed a 6 cm tear. I found it difficult to move, particularly on the backhand side. It was very frustrating to enter my second successive semi-final at the Australian Open with such a huge handicap.

I went up to Amir Takla, an Australian physiotherapist who had worked with me before and said, 'Amir, I want this title real bad! You have to make sure I can at least play the final.' Amir consulted his friend and colleague, Ivan Gutierrez, who was the physiotherapist of Lleyton Hewitt. Together, they came up with a plan.

'This will be very painful, Sania,' Amir said, 'but we can ensure that you are fit enough to play two more matches in this Australian Open.' He then went on to explain what they intended to do, and I must say it didn't excite me at all. Amir wanted to put a finger on the torn muscle and press it – a procedure intended to get the blood rushing to that part of the body and speed up recovery.

The treatment was more painful than anything I could have imagined in my worst nightmares. I almost passed out but miraculously, I felt better the next day. In fact, we had an easy outing in the semi-final against the Czech team of Iveta Benesova and Lukas

Dlouhy and stormed into our second successive Australian Open mixed doubles final.

Mahesh had reached the final in the men's doubles as well, partnering Mark Knowles, and I watched him face the Bryan brothers for the title a day before we were to play for the mixed doubles championship. It was an amazing match and the Bryans managed to beat the Indo-Bahamas duo in a very closely contested final. Mahesh was obviously rattled and I spent some time with him, along with the rest of his team, trying to help him recover. He may have won a handful of Grand Slam titles over the years but every loss in a final hurts. He still had another final to play, we consoled him.

As I entered the Rod Laver Arena to play the second Grand Slam final of my career, I felt a sense of déjà vu. We had been here exactly a year ago, in similar circumstances. My partner was the same and, once again, I had a physical impediment that threatened to slow me down. I was perhaps more nervous this time than in my first Grand Slam final. I was also concerned about Mahesh and any hangover from the narrow loss of the previous night. I needn't have worried. Champion that he is, Mahesh lifted himself admirably and we got off to a flying start against the Nathalie Dechy–Andy Ram combination, whom we had beaten in the semi-final the previous year.

Once the match started, nerves slipped away. We broke Ram's serve in the first game and then Mahesh held to give us a 2-0 lead. A couple of unforced errors and we were back on serve as Ram-Dechy held twice to move ahead 3-2. We then stepped it up in style, combining beautifully as I opened up the court with my ground strokes and Mahesh served and volleyed with authority.

I surprised myself with a few brilliant volleys and smashes which made Mahesh's father comment later that I 'played like a woman possessed'. Return of serve is a strength for both of us and we were on fire on all counts that day. We won the final 6-3, 6-1, totally outplaying our opponents.

I was a Grand Slam champion! Another childhood dream had come true! These are the moments you play tennis for. You strive for years to give yourself an opportunity to win a Slam and when you finally achieve your goal, it's the most uplifting moment of your life. I had seen a lot of players crying after winning a Grand Slam and had always wondered if I would too. Somehow that is not quite me but the joy I felt was intense. All the sacrifices, the hours of training, the pain and the losses, everything seemed worth it.

Victory felt even sweeter because my aunt Ruhina and her daughters who live in Melbourne were in attendance, as was my best friend, Lavraj, who was studying in the city at the time. He had watched me lose the previous year, but this time we had a Grand Slam title to celebrate.

Mahesh and I had taken care of each other off the court many times, through ups and downs, and that closeness has helped us on court. He has the happy knack of defusing a tense moment with a casual, witty comment but when we step on to the court, we are both quite intense. I was especially happy for Hesh, who had literally not slept after losing in the men's doubles final the day before.

We behaved like school kids as our troupe of Mahesh, Scott Davidoff, trainer Shayamal Vallabhjee, Dad and I went around Melbourne Park, clicking pictures while holding the trophy aloft. We also mingled with our supporters and took photographs with them, to their great joy and delight. Apart from that, the post-match dope tests and other logistics left hardly any time for celebrations. Before we knew it, we were on our way home.

We flew back to India and were greeted with a tumultuous reception at the airport in Mumbai. We walked out together with the trophy passing from one pair of hands to another. Later that evening, a huge crowd received me when I landed in Hyderabad. My mother had organized a celebration at home for close friends and relatives and the festivities carried on through the night.

A few months earlier, as I struggled with my wrist injury, I had wondered if I would ever be able to play competitive tennis again. Well, here I was – a Grand Slam champion and the first Indian woman to have achieved that feat. I had also become the youngest player from my country to win a Grand Slam title, at the age of twenty-two years and two months, surpassing Mahesh's record in the bargain. Heshy didn't seem to mind at all.

What more could I ask for? I had won the Australian Open while partnering my own countryman. It was an added bonus that he was a hero I had grown up admiring and now one of my closest friends.

27

HEARTBREAK TIME

I HAD FINISHED 2008 ranked 99 in the world and it seemed apparent to most critics that it was only a matter of days before I slipped out of the top-100 forever. However, the 2009 mixed doubles Australian Open title at the start of the year was inspirational and my singles performance improved significantly.

I was the runner-up in singles in Pattaya immediately after the Australian Open, losing in the final to Vera Zvonareva, ranked No. 5 at the time. We had devised a strategy to counter the Russian's backhand, which is her biggest strength. She packs a lot of punch, variation and consistency in her double-handed stroke. Playing cross-court meant I would be playing to her strength and going down the line was risky as Vera's ball was heavily spun. So I decided to play the ball back into the middle of the court, which would take away the acute angle that she was capable of employing with her next stroke. This would give me enough leeway to run around my backhand and use the brute power of my forehand to create some parity in our exchanges.

The first set was closely fought but Vera had the better rub of the green at critical moments before she jammed the pedal on me in the second set. However, the wins in the earlier rounds against a couple of top-50 players, Magdalena Rybarikova and homegrown veteran Tamarine Tanasugarn, had been very satisfying, as was the thrill of figuring in the final of a tournament that boasted a field which included the soon-to-be-world No. 1, Caroline Wozniacki.

After the tournament, I decided to travel to Las Vegas with the Adidas team to work with Andre Agassi's world-famous trainer, Gil Reyes. I soon realized he was an amazing man who had devised unique ways and built special machines for training the human body, especially aspiring professional athletes. Sorana Cirstea, Ana Ivanovic, Caroline Wozniacki and Fernando Verdasco were the other players who were working with Gil during that time and after a long, hard day of physical training and tennis, we would go out for dinner as a team, accompanied by our respective families. We even watched a couple of famous Las Vegas shows. It was great fun, but then something happened that made my trip to the city a roaring success – I ran into Steffi Graf, my childhood idol!

I would have to admit that Steffi Graf has been my all-time favourite since the time I was six years old and I remain her most ardent admirer even today. Steffi is a wonderful athlete who carries herself with dignity on and off the court. When she was at her peak, her forehand was probably one of the greatest the world had seen. Her backhand slice was venomous too, and set her up nicely to unwind the big forehand – a weapon that she used with deadly effect to annihilate scores of opponents of her generation.

I watched her practise a couple of times at Wimbledon, several years after her retirement, and was amazed to find that she had still not lost her touch on the forehand and the sliced backhand. I admired Steffi not only for the grace with which she dominated tennis during her era but also for the poise with which she had slipped into her new role as the wife of Andre Agassi and an adoring mother to their kids.

I had just finished my practice session with Sven Groeneveld and was leaving the tennis courts when I saw Steffi Graf coming towards us. I stared at her nervously, tongue-tied, not knowing what to do or say and wonder of wonders, it was the legend who introduced herself to me: 'Hey! I'm Steffi. How did the practice go, Sania?' she asked with a smile that was as bright as the desert sun.

'It was g-g-good!' I stammered, barely able to speak to the woman I had admired all my life.

'Why don't we practise together one of these days?' she said.

'Y-y-yes!' I mumbled with a weak smile.

We never got the opportunity to practise together, but just meeting my childhood hero was thrilling and totally made my day. It's a moment that I'll remember and cherish for the rest of my life.

*

I drove down from Las Vegas with Sven, his assistant 'Matsy', and Dad to Indian Wells for the next tournament. It was such a beautiful drive through the picturesque California desert. I did not go deep in the tournament in either Indian Wells or in Miami the following fortnight but in Charleston, I got the better of the precociously talented Bulgarian, Sesil Karatantcheva, which earned me the right to challenge Venus Williams. The American was in sublime form and led 6-1, 2-1 with a break up in the second set before the match turned on its head. I evened it out by winning the second set 6-3 and was sitting pretty after having broken her in the decider. But Venus played flawlessly from that point onwards to dispel any threats to her supremacy.

Sven Groeneveld, my coach at the time, is a thinker and extremely methodical in his ways. He was responsible for changing the action of my serve and I think it was a positive move that gave it a lot more reliability. I remember serving a bunch of double faults in my first round loss against Galina Voskoboeva at the French Open in 2009. With a week to go for the grass court season, Sven and I slogged it out on the artificial grass courts located just outside the main arena of Roland Garros. Sven had observed me for more than a year at close quarters. He believed I possessed one of the best overheads in women's tennis and yet, when I served, my body lacked balance. He worked towards incorporating the posture that I used for my overhead into my service action and it immediately had a positive impact.

I now began serving with a simplified motion and with my feet apart, instead of moving the right foot forward after tossing the ball, which was the more conventional thing to do. This gave me a three-pronged advantage over my earlier action. Since my toss has always tended to be a bit wayward, I now had a better chance of adjusting myself to the line and flight of the released ball as my body was better balanced, with a wider centre of gravity. Sven believed that my ball sense and racket head speed would adequately compensate for the loss of power that could occur due to the changed action and reduced movement. I think he was right.

Secondly, the improved body balance prevented the inadvertent dropping of my elbow to some extent. The new technique added to my consistency as I now made contact with the ball with my elbow held a little higher. Finally, taking away a few movements from the serve while simplifying it reduced the chances of committing basic errors.

I found the positivity that Sven exuded very refreshing. He would look for positives in the most difficult situations and even in the worst of losses and this transcended into my own thinking. His attitude helped me become more objectively analytical about my performances and enabled me to bounce back quicker from my losses.

The grass court season started well for me and I reached the semi-finals in Birmingham. Another couple of top-50 wins over the talented Russian, Anastasia Pavlyuchenkova, and British hope Anne Keothavong added to my growing confidence. I had also got the better of veterans Tatiana Poutchek and Melinda Czink to make it four straight wins on grass.

Wimbledon, therefore, began with a lot of promise. It was exciting to beat a former top-15 player, Anna-Lena Groenefeld of Germany in round one but, disappointingly, I could not keep the momentum going. Sorana Cirstea of Romania played an absolutely sensational second-round match against me that put paid to my aspirations of going deep in the draw.

That year I won the Lexington ITF title, beating top seed Julie Coin in straight sets in the final, and then finished as the runner-up in Vancouver the following week. The competition was a rung below the best in both these tournaments but strategically, I was looking for more matches and more wins at that stage of my career and these victories did no harm to my confidence and ranking.

I also had a decent run in doubles in 2009 with my best performance coming at Ponte Vedra Beach, USA, on green clay. I won the title with Taipei's Chia-Jung Chuang as my partner. It was a strong field and we overcame Bethanie Mattek-Sands and Nadia Petrova in the quarter-final before beating the top seeds, Kveta Peschke and Lisa Raymond, in a thrilling final.

*

Towards the early part of the year though, I struggled a bit in my personal life. I was briefly engaged to a college mate, Mohammed Sohrab Mirza, who also happened to be the son of Dad's friends. I had known Sohrab for a long time and we moved in the same circles. While we weren't particularly close ourselves, we often met at parties and get-togethers with our common gang.

It was during my injury lay-off in 2008, which can often be a cruel and vulnerable period for any athlete, that I had started spending more time with Sohrab. It was a tough period for me. My wrist injury had left me despondent, swinging between despair and hopelessness. I couldn't even hold my phone, or eat without help, or wash my own hair. Playing tennis seemed a distant possibility and I was close to slipping into depression. Around this time I started looking forward to a new chapter in my life without realizing it.

Everything seemed to fit perfectly – Sohrab was a family friend belonging to my community from my own city, which meant I could remain close to my parents. A few months down the line, we thought getting engaged was the right thing to do. But I guess some things are not meant to be. We tried our best to make it work but it soon dawned on us that being good friends and compatible life partners were two different things altogether.

Around this time, something else happened to affect me quite deeply. One of my closest friends from childhood, Arif Hyder, was involved in a serious motorbike accident in September 2009. The son of my parents' very dear friends, Arif had travelled with me as a junior to several all-India tennis tournaments. He was a strong, talented player but had decided to concentrate on academics and later became totally engrossed in his family business. Arif was always so full of life. He loved food like I did and had a fascination for fast cars and bikes. He had been over the moon when I won the Australian Open earlier that year in January and had led the delegation of friends, relatives and fans that received me on my triumphant return at the airport in Hyderabad.

The accident was serious and the doctors who first saw him were pessimistic about his chances of recovery. I was in Japan, playing in a tournament, when I heard the news. I was devastated. I saw him in hospital for the first time a few days later and tennis suddenly seemed so insignificant in the larger scheme of things. Here was one of my childhood friends, in a semi-coma, barely able to lift a finger on his own.

It was disheartening to see a buddy in that state, but Arif was always a fighter. With the Almighty's help and a lot of loving support from his family, he has defied the judgement of medical specialists. Today, he has come a long way. Having undergone about half a dozen complicated surgeries, he has successfully begun a new life. He has made us all proud and his tremendous grit and willpower are an inspiration for all those who have been associated with him in any capacity.

Arif and I had spent memorable times together, along with my other great friends, Lavraj and Anil Yadav, when we were growing up. We were known as the 'Boys Gang'! They were my seniors in St Mary's College and we were inseparable friends. Arif's accident brought us all together once again after we had drifted away a bit – each of us having got immersed in our own careers. Lavraj is a very successful builder while 'Anna' (as we affectionately called Anil) is from a political family and nurtures ambitions to follow the path of his father. I hope he goes from strength to strength in his career but to us, he will always remain our Anna!

28

FINDING LOVE

FOR SOME STRANGE reason, even as a young girl, I had this notion that I would be married by the time I was twenty-three years old. I was quite an orthodox person, still am in many ways. I thought I would stop playing tennis once I got married, and have a child by the time I was twenty-seven or twenty-eight. It was just how I pictured my life. All my friends today are married and have children. So maybe it was also the kind of life that everyone around me was planning when I was growing up and I had made a similar timeline in my mind too. But as you grow up, you learn that life does not always turn out the way you expect it to.

After the break-up with Sohrab, the chances of my adolescent plans working out seemed to have considerably reduced. Soon after my twenty-third birthday, I threw myself into tennis as I struggled with another comeback in Australia, following the chronic wrist impairment. It was here, in the beautiful little city of Hobart in early 2010, that my life went through another dramatic twist.

That evening, Dad, trainer Len and I walked into the familiar Indian restaurant that was located on the waterfront a few hundred yards away from The Old Woolstore Hotel, where we were lodged for one of the tournaments leading up to the year's first Grand Slam. The Pakistan cricket team was scheduled to play a Test match against Australia in a couple of days' time and we were pleasantly surprised to find some of the players enjoying their dinner at the same restaurant.

A little later, former Pakistan captain Shoaib Malik entered, looking for a table, and came towards the corner where we were sitting. He said hello to me and then approached our table to pay his respects to my father. I had met Shoaib earlier, though very briefly. A journalist had introduced us in the gym of a hotel in New Delhi, a few years back, when Pakistan was playing a series in India. On another occasion, I had seen him in the breakfast area of a hotel in Mohali, where I had gone to watch India play Pakistan in a one-day match.

When Shoaib expressed interest in watching me play the next evening, I arranged some tickets for him. He came, accompanied by a couple of his teammates. After the match, my father invited the boys for dinner at the same Indian restaurant and while the others had a prior engagement, Shoaib accepted the offer.

We stayed in touch on the phone while travelling for our matches to different cities in Australia. The first thing that drew me towards him was his simplicity. He seemed totally unaffected by his fame – he was, after all, his country's former cricket captain and a senior member of the current team. Soon we were talking about almost everything under the sun and realized that we got along rather well. However, love was still a fair distance away.

A month later, I was travelling for the Dubai Open and Shoaib was captaining Pakistan on those very dates in a one-day series against England in the same city. He had been reinstated as the skipper of his country's one-day team for this series. Perhaps the Almighty was throwing us both together, facilitating an unlikely match. Shoaib met my mother and she too got along well with him.

A couple of months later, Shoaib asked me to marry him. He is not a dramatic person and his proposal was as simple as it can get. He told me that regardless of when it happened, he wanted to marry me and he was going to tell his mother about his decision. I liked this side of him a lot, as I am a no-fuss person myself.

Many months later, when we were finally married and enjoying a pleasant evening together, I wondered out loud to him, 'Imagine if you hadn't come to that restaurant that day. We would have never even met.' That's when he told me it wasn't entirely by chance that he had stepped into the restaurant in Hobart that fateful evening.

One of his teammates, who was already in the restaurant, had called Shoaib to tell him that I was dining there. Shoaib, who had earlier decided against eating out, came rushing. He said, 'This time I was determined to get your number.' We still joke about it, knowing it wasn't just 'chance' that brought us together.

The decision to get married came naturally to me. I was relatively conservative when it came to marriage. I didn't think it was important for us to date for a long period before deciding. Also, it was getting more difficult for us to keep our relationship under wraps. We were both recognizable faces. We did manage for a while though, which is why when it became public, it was a shock to everyone.

I spoke to my mom about Shoaib and he, in turn, spoke to his mother. In March, his family, including his mother, sister, brother-in-law and their two kids accompanied Shoaib to India and were guests in our house. Three days later, a formal proposal was made and my parents accepted, though they did voice their concerns about Shoaib's nationality.

I was conscious of the fact that Shoaib belonged to a country that had serious political differences with us. But I had grown up on the tennis circuit where I had shared close friendships over the years with people of diverse religions, races and backgrounds from scores of different countries across the globe. I think this experience had broadened my horizons to the extent that I could comfortably embrace relationships on a personal level beyond these constraints. As athletes, you forget such boundaries.

The one thing that I did speak to Shoaib about, right at the beginning, was his view of my career. He had no problem with me playing after marriage but I wanted him to confirm this with his family too, well before we tied the knot. His mother was quite clear and open-minded about it and to this date, they are as proud of me and my career as my own family is. The fact that there have been athletes in Shoaib's family perhaps helped them understand my life and its pressures too.

That, in fact, is one of the best aspects of our relationship. As athletes, we were both used to travelling extensively for work and being away from home for long periods. We had lived that life for years and were mentally prepared to be away from each other for long stretches. Knowing how to handle the distance and long phases away was going to help both of us sustain the relationship.

*

The year 2009 had turned out to be reasonably successful considering I had gone through a tricky wrist surgery. The results could have been even better had it not been for the chronic pain that kept recurring. I played with the help of painkillers for as long as I could, but sometimes it would become unbearable. The spectre of this ugly injury, which I feared would end my career, continued to cast its shadow in the early part of 2010 as well. Professionally I was struggling and there was nothing to write home about all through the Australian leg. I crashed out in the first round at four consecutive events, starting in Hobart and ending in Dubai in February. The nagging pain forced me to take an indefinite break, perhaps the toughest yet, because this time I had no idea if I would return. This, more than anything else, created extreme pressure on me, especially with the Commonwealth and Asian Games lined up later in the year. I was almost resigned to my fate. Struggling for over a year with the pain post-surgery, it really felt like the end of my career was near.

With Shoaib and myself both out of action for different reasons, we decided it would be best to get married as soon as we could, to put the enforced break to good use. I immersed myself in wedding plans. It enabled me to take my mind off the injury and helped me stay buoyant. It was great fun, planning and working out the details of our future life together. We decided to make Dubai our home as it seemed well-suited from several angles, including its strategic location within striking distance of both our countries.

Shoaib was scheduled to play a series of matches in the Bangladesh Premier League, to which he was already committed, and he planned to come to India afterwards. We decided to announce our wedding once he reached Hyderabad. But we had not bargained for what followed. The days preceding our wedding turned out to be the most tense and gruelling time that a bride, her groom and their families could ever go through.

Our plan to keep things under wraps till Shoaib reached India did not quite work out. Murmurs about the impending wedding broke out in the media a few days before his arrival. After all, it was only a matter of time before the news of the marriage of two well-known sports personalities from either side of the border was leaked through some source or the other.

Shoaib arrived in Hyderabad from Dubai on 4 April. He tried to hide his face as he made his way out of the airport. There were still a lot of people around who could have recognized him. Dad and I waited for him in the car park while one of my uncles went in to receive him.

None of us had any idea how to deal with the potentially explosive situation. We were all just coming up with strategies to best avoid any drama as we went along. Shoaib did his best to avoid being recognized, but he completely forgot that the bag he was carrying had 'Pakistan Cricket Team – Shoaib Malik' emblazoned on it in bold letters!

The moment my uncle saw this, he literally jumped on the bag to ensure that nobody noticed what was written on it. And that's pretty much how the madness unfolded over the next few days, in this most tiring, emotionally sapping, frustrating, and sometimes hilarious period of our lives.

The situation took an ugly turn when a woman made allegations against my would-be husband and certain sections of the media on both sides of the border took it upon themselves to discuss threadbare the intricate details of our personal relationship. In India, a 'media trial' erupted as newsmen competed savagely with one another to tear the prospective 'foreign groom' to shreds. Several proved themselves to be totally insensitive to the repercussions on my personal life as they jostled with each other in their quest for TRPs. Without knowing the truth, they did everything they could to break my alliance with a man I loved.

It would not be wrong to say that for almost two weeks the media went berserk. About two hundred newsmen armed with cameras and microphones, files and pens, camped outside our house and hounded every guest and family member as they entered or left. A dozen satellite vans were parked in the lane, beaming inconsequential footage of the house and visitors. Cameras were fixed on all sides and were recording round the clock. Camera crews had bagged strategic positions on buildings around the house to gain a 360-degree perspective. If the curtains at a window moved even an inch, exposing one of my family members or me doing mundane chores in the house, some news channels thought it important to telecast the image to viewers with super-imaginative interpretations. It was totally bizarre and unexpected!

On one of those days, amidst all the madness, my father got a frantic call from a relative who sounded hysterical. 'Is Sania wearing a green T-shirt?' he questioned. When my dad answered in the affirmative, he almost screamed, 'Draw your curtains! There are cameras fixed on the next-door building that's under construction and news channels are showing her live right now!'

I did not see sunlight for about ten days. All the windows, even the small vents in the bathrooms, had to be covered. Even the smallest of peepholes were being used by the media to beam images. Going out to the balcony for a breather was asking for trouble.

A week into the frenzy, we decided we'd had enough. We needed some fresh air. So, in the middle of the night, we took the risk of going out for ice cream. We thought the crowd of media persons would have thinned out by then and even the reporters would be too tired to stay vigilant. But we were mistaken. We were chased throughout, filmed even as we bought and ate our treats inside our car.

A contingent of the press even tailed my father when he went to the mosque for Friday prayers. He stopped them from carrying their photography and recording equipment into the mosque but a couple of them stealthily followed him inside and stood on either side while he prayed. They had the audacity to pull out a small, hidden microphone to ask him ridiculous questions even as he was praying.

Filth and muck began to be thrown around publicly. A few opportunistic media men believed they had struck a goldmine and tried to make the most of it by blowing up personal issues without any concern for truth, decency or propriety. To my shocked disbelief, they found some willing allies in the city's social circle, who jumped at the opportunity to be seen and heard on television. Juicy appendages were tastelessly added to create a demonic image of my would-be husband. Every effort was now being made to package the story in a manner that would keep it alive and kicking in the interest of grabbing more and more eyeballs.

Almost a week had gone by since the media had jumped into our lives. Every little detail had already been discussed threadbare and beamed out live. Then a section of the media tried to raise a storm about the fact that Shoaib was living with us in our house before marriage. How could he stay with the prospective bride in her house? Was that even allowed under Islam? These were the questions thrown around with an absolute lack of sensitivity. Once again, clerics were asked to comment on camera on the propriety of our living together, which was a complete misrepresentation of the facts. Shoaib was in the house along with both our families and the two of us were on different floors in our four-level home. But that did not matter to those raising these questions in the media. In the days leading up to my wedding, some men and women with the power of the pen or the microphone seemed to lose their bearings.

However, once this new angle had stirred up enough controversy, with more and more people expressing their opinions, the elders decided that Shoaib should move into a hotel before the day of the wedding to put a stop to the nonsensical debates in the media.

The question was, how could we manage to get him away without attracting the attention of the media camped outside?

Once again, one of my uncles sprang into action. He went outside, in full view of the media, shouting loudly into his phone, pretending to have an ugly, and possibly juicy, fight. As the journalists started converging around him in the hope of gaining some vital information, Shoaib slipped into the small car that was usually used for household work like buying groceries. My uncle kept the media herd away from our main gate while Shoaib lay down in the car to hide himself and was quietly whisked away to check into a hotel.

Amidst all the madness, we somehow still managed to have the fun that a wedding brings along. While the media was pacing relentlessly outside our house, my closest friends and family members were busy practising their dance steps. Rakshanda Khan, a well-known TV personality, has been a close friend of mine for years. We met at the lounge of an airport when I was still very young. We were both accompanied by our mothers. We hit it off instantly and that friendship has endured till today although we don't get to meet each other often. She performed a 'number' during one of the wedding functions, as did Neha Dhupia, my Bollywood friend who had come to Hyderabad for the wedding.

My family and I can look back now and laugh, shaking our heads in disbelief at the crazy happenings and the turmoil. It was a near miracle that amidst all this chaos, we managed to retain our sanity. But there is no denying that many around us, and especially the media, had lost all perspective. Several of them failed their professional ethics completely by creating havoc in our personal lives. They were guilty of not only trying to break up my marriage but also of indulging in slander without any notion of the truth.

Many within the family had started to worry if the wedding would actually take place. Some of them advised us to postpone it. Shoaib would have none of it. He said, 'I came here to get married to you and I am not leaving until we get married.'

At one point, closer to the wedding, my mother had a complete breakdown. She just could not handle the tension any more and started to cry hysterically. Despite the enormous pressure put on them, my parents had somehow managed to make everything work, maintaining a remarkably stoic and controlled appearance. They could barely sleep in the run-up to the wedding. Having them disintegrate would have surely sent things spiralling further down for us. But as my dad says, 'This is just what we do really well. The Mirza family can laugh its way through any problem while maintaining a steely resolve.' There is no way I could have gone through it all without their relentless support.

Finally, on 12 April 2010, a boy from Pakistan married a girl from India for love amidst an unprecedented media frenzy. As I headed for the biggest occasion of my life, dressed in my bridal finery, my personal car was chased by an army of media men in vans, all the way from my house to Hotel Taj Krishna, where the guests had already gathered for the nikah. It was an intimate function with just a handful of close relatives and friends. To avoid any untoward incident, I was made to enter from the service door at the back of the hotel and through the kitchen area. This was probably another first in the annals of wedding history! Once we were safely inside, the ceremony went off beautifully. This was followed by a sangeet the next day and a formal reception a day later.

It had been a trial by fire but the drama ended on a happy note and we were finally man and wife, enjoying the tranquil peace of the evening on the balcony of our hotel room. 'So many people have wronged you. I shudder to think of how they can live with themselves and face the Almighty when the time comes,' I said to Shoaib at one point, holding back the tears that threatened to flow down my cheeks. 'But we need to get on with our lives now and, as in all other matters, leave the final judgement to God.'

'May Allah forgive them,' Shoaib said, with no malice in his voice, and I smiled back at him, knowing I had made the right choice.

29

CWG AND ASIAN GAMES 2010

THE CHRONIC PAIN in my wrist had forced me to stop playing tennis for almost four months, perhaps the longest break I had ever taken from the game. Before throwing in the towel I had tried virtually every kind of treatment I possibly could in my efforts to cure the troubled wrist. I had even used Korean needle therapy on the advice of some family friends.

The therapist was based in New Delhi and I would travel with Mom to the capital city, where I stayed at the residence of one of my mother's best friends, Sumita Dawra, while undergoing treatment. The prick of the needles was painful but we spent a few relaxed weeks, enjoying Sumita Aunty's hospitality – it felt like a home away from home. The needle therapy helped, but the relief was shortlived. The pain recurred and ultimately, I had to stop playing on the circuit.

I had used the enforced break from tennis to get married and when I did attempt a comeback, winning matches was more difficult than I had imagined. It is not easy to return to the competitive world of professional tennis after a prolonged period away from the game. However, I was glad to at least be back on the court, this time with no pain in my wrist. The break from the game seemed to have done wonders after every other kind of treatment had failed to provide relief.

I struggled for results on my return in June, in the run-up to

Wimbledon. I had managed to stay at a ranking inside the top-100 despite the break but slipped about thirty places soon after returning. At Wimbledon I ran into Germany's rising star, Angelique Kerber, in the first round. Later that year, I won three qualifying matches to make the US Open main draw, eventually losing to twentieth seed Anastasia Pavlyuchenkova in the second round.

My eyes were set at this time on the Commonwealth Games (CWG) coming up in New Delhi in October. Winning a medal at the Games at home became an obsession and it was this burning desire that kept me going in extremely trying circumstances. It was the first time that tennis was being included in the CWG. I had performed creditably whenever I played for India in multi-discipline events but on this occasion, due to the long injury break, I did not have a lot of matches under my belt. I was also worried about my wrist and wondered if the pain would come back to haunt me again. The 'experts' had written me off completely at this point of time but I was determined to make them eat their words. Shoaib was in Delhi to cheer me on and the fans were delighted to see him in person, rooting for me.

I had an easy first round in singles against Brittany Teei of Cook Islands and then played a good match to get the better of Marina Erakovic of New Zealand. The Kiwi is a very talented tennis player and the huge crowd at the centre court of the R.K. Khanna Stadium helped me get past a sticky opponent. I then went on to beat Olivia Rogowska of Australia, after having lost the first set, to march triumphantly into the final of the 2010 Commonwealth Games and in the process, assured myself of a medal.

Russia's Anastasia Rodionova had been cleared to play for Australia less than a year ago. She was the top seed and I looked forward to playing against her for the gold medal. It turned out to be a match worthy of a final. 'Roddy' was on a high and playing probably the best tennis of her career. I had struggled in the months prior to the CWG but the home crowd lifted my spirits and helped me raise my game.

Roddy took the opening set and I came back strongly to win the second at 6-2. I took an early lead in the decider before the Australian struck back, breaking me twice, and then served for the match at 5-3. I was not finished yet and played some inspired tennis to take the third set into a tie-breaker. The crowd was hysterical at this point. I gave it everything I had but went down fighting after saving three match points. It broke my heart to miss out on a gold medal so narrowly.

Anastasia was magnanimous in victory and generous with her post-match comments. 'Sania is a great player. I knew I had to play my best. It was a high quality match and it's a great feeling to be part of a great final,' she said. The entire Australian team, which inherently loves a fighter, lavishly praised my effort but that day I would have given anything to be able to exchange my silver medal for the gold that I had so agonisingly missed out on. I went out to the poolside behind the players' lounge in the stadium and wept bitterly in the dark. I did not even realize how long I was there alone, just letting it all out. It was one of my most painful losses ever. My parents let me be for half an hour before coming to help me get up.

When I look back at my performance, it is gratifying to know that I gave it all I had as an athlete. The pain of a loss gradually subsides and what is left are ecstatic memories of a thrilling battle. However, at the precise moment when one loses on court, especially on such a stage, one is left heartbroken and depressed.

A couple of days later, Rushmi Chakravarthi and I unexpectedly won the bronze in the women's doubles and my second medal for India in the 2010 Commonwealth Games provided some consolation for the second-round loss that Leander and I suffered in the mixed.

I had to pick myself up soon after the crushing loss in the women's singles final as the Guangzhou Asian Games were to follow almost immediately. I was still unseeded but the run at the CWG had given me newfound confidence before my third straight Asiad. I defeated Chan Wing-Yau in the first round of the women's singles, then beat Zhang Shuai, the sixth seed, and once again outplayed the seasoned Thai, Tamarine Tanasugarn, to assure myself of a bronze medal without dropping a set. But I went down fighting in the semi-final against Akgul Amanmuradova after winning the first set in a tie-break.

No one had expected our scratch mixed doubles team of the inexperienced Vishnu Vardhan and myself to do well in Guangzhou. With Leander Paes, Mahesh Bhupathi and Rohan Bopanna opting to play in the ATP event instead of the Asian Games, Vishnu and I conjured up a few amazing victories to take us to the final which we lost narrowly to Yung-Jan Chan and Yang Tsung-hua of Taipei. We settled for a silver medal – a feat that had seemed very unlikely when we started our campaign.

With a silver and a bronze at the Guangzhou Asian Games, I had now rounded off my personal tally of medals won for India to a dozen in various multi-discipline international events. For me, each of these medals shines with a moving personal story that I take special pride in and this, as much as anything else, has made me feel complete and fulfilled in my career.

*

Shifting focus to the tour and intent on improving my rankings, I played in the Al Habtoor Tennis Challenge in Dubai with probably one of the toughest fields that I have competed in at the Challenger level. It was virtually like playing a WTA event. I enjoyed what proved to be a very successful tournament for me, beating the fast improving Ksenia Pervak to kick off my campaign. I then knocked out the No. 1-seeded top-30 player Julia Goerges before overcoming Evgeniya Rodina en route to the final. I went on to beat the second seed Bojana Jovanovski of Serbia for the title.

The Australian Open, in my favourite city of Melbourne, was my next big assignment. Here I got the opportunity to play against Justine Henin, a player I respected. I had won three qualifying matches to earn the right to play the petite Belgian who owns the greatest single-handed backhand the world of women's tennis has ever seen. Taking a set from Henin is one of the sweet memories of my career although

I did miss out on the chance to beat one of the revered players of my era. She upped her game in the third set after I had missed a crucial opportunity to go up a break in the second.

The next few months were nothing short of a massive struggle to try and get back to my best. I had to work hard for each and every win that came my way to gradually break back into the top-100 and reach as high as 58 before Wimbledon in June.

30

STRIKING FORM AGAIN

MY DOUBLES GAME picked up remarkably in 2011 and the results were stunning. My new partner Elena Vesnina and I came together quite by accident. We were both playing in New Zealand in the run-up to the Australian Open, where I had committed to play with Renata Voracova. Vesnina was looking for a doubles partner because Vera Zvonoreva, with whom she had been playing, felt she needed to focus on her singles game for a few months. 'Ves' and I had been good friends from our junior days but somehow the opportunity to play together had never presented itself until then. We decided to start with the Middle Eastern events in Dubai and Doha and take it from there, depending on the results.

We did reasonably well in our first two tournaments and agreed to continue our partnership on the hard courts of USA. It was here that we came into our own. Ves and I won the prestigious Indian Wells tournament, my first premier level title, and followed it up by winning in Charleston, although we suffered an early exit in Miami. We beat the American team of Bethanie Mattek-Sands and Meghann Shaughnessy in the finals of both the tournaments.

We had done well enough in the four months to be rewarded with the seventh seeding in our first Grand Slam as a team, at Roland Garros. We faced the Russian doubles combination of Ekaterina Makarova and Vera Dushevina in the first round and despite playing a shaky match, pulled it off quite comfortably in the second set after winning the first via a tie-breaker.

We were a cheerful duo at our post-match dinner that night. We felt that it augured well to have won on a day when Ves and I were both a bit off-colour. Winning a doubles Grand Slam requires a total of six wins in a row and it's not possible for a team to be at its best on all of those match days. The key was to be able to win on the days when we were below par and we had just done that.

I had beaten Kristina Barrois in singles earlier in the week and the German was looking to avenge her loss when she played us in doubles, partnering Johanna Larsson. But Ves and I gave an improved display to win in straight sets. We had a tough draw and now faced the eleventh-seeded Spanish clay court specialists in the form of Maria Jose Martinez Sanchez and Anabel Medina Garrigues. We would have backed ourselves against the consistent left-right combination on any other surface, but on the red clay of Paris we needed to fire on all cylinders, which we did! We never allowed the Spanish pair to settle down, winning easily for a loss of just five games in the match.

The top-seeded pair of Flavia Pennetta of Italy and Argentine Gisela Dulko were our opponents in the quarter-final stage. Apart from being the No.1 team in the world, the pair relished playing on clay, having been brought up on that surface in their respective countries. We played a tremendous match that day to overpower the top seeds 6-0, 7-5. Remarkably, this time too, we lost a mere five games and stormed into the semis without dropping a single set.

In my opinion, Lisa Raymond is one of the greatest doubles players of my era. She was playing with Liezel Huber and the fourth seeds had quietly made their way into the semi-finals. With four impressive wins under our belt, Ves and I were playing commanding tennis and it was this resounding confidence that enabled us to play a pulsating match against the seasoned and daunting American team. We held our nerve on most of the big points and won 6-4 in the third set, marching triumphantly into the final of the Grand Slam.

The unseeded Czech team of Andrea Hlavackova and Lucie

Hradecka had sliced through the list of big names in their half of the draw. They went on to upset Yaroslava Shvedova and Vania King in the semi-final to join us in the battle for clay supremacy. In the run-up to the French Open, Lucie had partnered me in Strasbourg as our respective partners took a break before the Slam and we had been unceremoniously beaten in the first round of the WTA tournament by the German team of Angelique Kerber and Katarzyna Piter. Who would have thought that two weeks later she and I would be fighting it out against each other for a Grand Slam title!

It all came down to an anti-climactic end for us, though. We lost the final in straight sets and the disappointment of missing a realistic chance of winning a Grand Slam wasn't easy to cope with. I had personally missed my greatest opportunity yet of owning a French Open title, but I was determined to be back. In 2008, Mahesh Bhupathi and I were the runners-up at the Aussie Open and we had gone on to win the following year. Maybe the runners-up trophy at Roland Garros in 2011 would be a forerunner to the title the following year, I consoled myself.

My good form in doubles continued and we made it to the semi-finals on grass at Wimbledon. To add to this, Rohan Bopanna and I reached the quarter-finals of the mixed doubles to make it a very successful Grand Slam.

The US hard court season was a little disappointing but we were still in with a chance to qualify among the top four teams for the championships that are held at the end of the year. A strong performance at the US Open would seal our spot, although we still had a few more tournaments to play in Asia where we could earn big points to improve our ranking. But this was not to be as we played Iveta Benesova and Barbora Strycova in the third round at Flushing Meadows and lost a close battle.

I had been playing continuously for a little over a year now since my comeback in the summer of 2010. Unbelievably, I had played more than 150 matches during the twelve-month period before Wimbledon. The reason for this excessive workload was simple. As my singles ranking had dropped due to the injury break, I had to play the qualifying rounds and then win a few more matches in the main draws of several tournaments. In doubles, I had been having a phenomenal year and played four to five matches every week. I also thought I had the best chance to win a Grand Slam in mixed doubles and did not want to miss out on that opportunity in the majors. Besides this, I played in the Fed Cup for India and participated in two or more events each in the Commonwealth Games and the Asian Games.

I knew I badly needed a break and was planning to take a few weeks off after the US Open when an injury flared up again. Towards the end of the third round match against Benesova-Strycova, I felt a sudden, stabbing pain in my left knee, which had troubled me for a while, and I instantly knew it was something serious. I did complete the match despite some discomfort but the problem was diagnosed as a tear in the meniscus and surgery was the only recourse. This put paid to our chances of playing in the year-end championships and, in fact, signalled an early end to my season.

Despite my modest performances in singles, I still managed to finish 2011 comfortably in the top-100 for the sixth time in my career. However, I knew that coming back from my third surgery was going to be extremely difficult, if not impossible. I could not help but look back at the series of injuries and comebacks I had endured already, each of them at a crucial stage in my career. To go through that all over again, after having had my wrist and both knees opened up by surgeons within a span of about four and a half years, was not an encouraging thought. Once again I was left despondent over the ominous signs that seemed to spell the end of my career.

31

GOODBYE TO SINGLES

By the time I was ready to board the flight to Auckland to play in the run-up tournament to the 2012 Australian Open, I was striking the ball well but I could see that my knees were going to trouble me all the way. I was thinking now about the option of quitting singles if forced to, as it no longer made sense to risk another surgery by continuing to push my body. However, before taking the final call, I wanted to give it my best shot.

Considering that I had been out of action for almost four months, I did phenomenally well at the Australian Open, reaching the semi-finals of the women's and mixed doubles, although I lost my first-round singles match to Tsvetana Pironkova. The semi-final showing enabled me to reach my then career-best ranking of seven in the world in doubles.

Soon after the year's first Grand Slam, I headed to Shenzhen, China for the Fed Cup. My performance in the three matches that I played there will remain one of the highlights of my career for several reasons. Four years earlier, I had played my part in a memorable encounter against Hong Kong that saved India from being demoted. In the 2012 edition of the Fed Cup, India played Hong Kong again in the play-off – this time for promotion to Group 1, and I was obliged to take centre stage again.

Rutuja Bhosale, Prerna Bhambri, Sharmada Balu and Isha Lakhani were part of the Indian team. I was still recovering from a quad injury that I had picked up during my doubles semi-final at the Australian Open and coach Enrico Piperno chose the others for the easier ties. One of the ten competing countries in our zone was to be promoted and things began to heat up as we confronted Philippines for a place in the play-off.

We were locked 1-all after Rutuja won her singles and Prerna lost hers. Isha and I played the deciding doubles and won easily at 6-0, 6-1. This earned us the right to challenge Hong Kong in another significant encounter in the play-off.

Rutuja lost her singles and I went in to face Zhang Ling with India 0-1 down. I had played just two singles matches in the last five months and was yet to record my first singles win post-surgery. I was rusty to begin with and lost the first set 5-7 to the No. 1 player from Hong Kong before I found my rhythm in the nick of time. I won the next two sets 6-0, 6-1 to bring India back to parity.

Isha and I played the deciding doubles again and I had to use all my experience to take us to a thrilling 5-7, 6-1, 7-5 victory that earned India a promotion. I had won three vital matches within twenty-four hours and each of these victories had been crucial for India's success in the Fed Cup. It was an extremely satisfying feeling.

In the next three months, I struggled for consistent results in singles, although I scored some good wins along the way. The continuing pain and unreliability of my left knee was beginning to take its toll on me. Whenever I played a long match, my knee would swell up. Then, as I subconsciously started putting more pressure on my other leg, the right knee that had undergone surgery five years ago began to swell up as well. My right wrist had lost some of its movement following the surgery in 2008 and now, after the lapse of a few years, it began to hurt again, especially when I was stretched on the forehand side.

When I had problems with injuries in the early part of my career, it was because I was unfit. Since then, I had worked extremely hard to attain international standards of fitness. But every time I got injured, the media was quick to shrug it off as my lack of fitness. What they did not know was that I had to deal with a condition in my bones which is a form of chronic arthritis called sensivitis, found generally in people of an advanced age. I had very lax joints, making them hypermobile, which put me at high risk for this ailment. If I hadn't been an athlete, it may not have mattered so much but since I played tennis, the condition exerted extreme pressure on my joints. In fact, the reason why my body showed signs of this ailment early in life was because of the wear-and-tear it had endured while playing tennis for nearly two decades. My joints were being pounded and abused on a daily basis. I had begun to live with pain and I could sense I was fighting a losing battle.

After a long singles match, apart from having to deal with a swollen knee, my wrist, back and ankles would be crying out for rest. Some critics think I took the 'easy' way out by retiring from singles when I still had a few years left, but they obviously did not know about the pain I routinely endured. I fought back three times after surgery, apart from getting over a number of serious muscle injuries in various parts of my body.

After having competed at the highest level, finding the motivation to return to playing in the smaller $25,000 ITF tournaments was tough. But I had done just that every time my ranking plunged due to a long break from the game post-surgery. I was not awarded too many wild-card entries at the WTA level and the only recourse was to play the smaller tournaments in order to get my ranking back up.

After trying hard for months in 2012, I had to take the tough call. I was still in the top-100 in singles but I knew I would have to realign my goals. That was the only way I could play tennis for a few more years and I loved the game too much to give it up completely. Considering what I had endured, I knew it was no longer a question of 'if' another serious joint injury would strike but 'when'.

I was also under considerable pressure to try and maintain my top-10 ranking in doubles in order to qualify for the upcoming London Olympics. I knew that if I continued to play with my troubled knees in both formats of the game, I would not survive at this level for more than a few months. The specialist doctors that I consulted were quite clear in their assessment. If I wished to prolong my career on the circuit, I needed to make some adjustments.

I picked and chose the singles events that I played. Then, after considerable thought and with a heavy heart, I decided that I would play the last two singles tournaments of my career in Brussels and Eastbourne before shifting my focus entirely to doubles. As it turned out, I had a superb tournament in the Belgian city famous for its chocolates. I not only won the 14th doubles title of my career (this time with Bethanie Mattek-Sands) but also scored three fluent singles wins over Yuliya Beygelzimer, Anastasia Rodionova and Lesia Tsurenko. Amazingly, I recorded a 6-0, 6-0 win in one of the last singles victories of my career on tour and that too, against Tsurenko – a player ranked just around the top-100 at that juncture. It had been a long time since I double-bageled an opponent and it gave me a sense of sweet satisfaction, given the circumstances.

I knew that I still had the skills and the game to compete against the best singles players in the business but my body was now too battered to carry on in this unforgiving format. Ten years of professional tennis, competing in singles and doubles, had taken their toll on me and the writing was on the wall. It was finally time to move on.

My goal changed to becoming the No. 1 doubles player in the world. The focus would now be on winning as many Grand Slams as possible. It was the start of a new journey. Of course, there are occasions when I still miss playing singles but it was the best choice I could have made at the time, setting aside my ego. It was certainly one of the hardest career decisions I ever had to make, but looking back today, I am convinced that I made the right choice.

32

STARRING AT ROLAND GARROS

IF ONE GOES through the draw of a mixed doubles event in a Grand Slam, one can be forgiven for reeling under the weight of all those heavy-duty names – of champions past and present. Almost every other team has at least one player who is a Grand Slam winner in men's, women's or mixed doubles and there are a few singles champions as well. It was an equally awe-inspiring field in the 2012 mixed doubles event of the French Open. Even though Mahesh and I were seeded seventh, with Max Mirnyi and Liezel Huber as the top seeds, the draw included Bob Bryan with Serena Williams, Mike Bryan with Kveta Peschke, Leander Paes with Elena Vesnina, Daniel Nestor with Nadia Petrova and Nenad Zimonjic with Katarina Srebotnik, amongst a galaxy of other past champions.

The Indian team for the London Olympics was to be announced soon after the Grand Slam and Hesh and I both felt we had the best chance of winning a medal if we played together. We had done well in the past and if we could put up a strong showing in Paris, there was no way the selection committee could split our winning combination. But for now, we were playing in a Grand Slam and winning a second title with Mahesh was my prime focus.

We played the American pair of Eric Butorac and Raquel Kops-Jones in the first round and beat them with consummate ease in straight sets. The French team of Nicolas Devilder and Virginie

Razzano was next and inspired by a partisan home crowd, the duo put up quite a fight. We lost the first set before digging deep in a third set super tie-break that we won 10-6.

The tournament was only just beginning to warm up and it was time to take on the bigger teams. Few can claim to be better than the Mike Bryan–Kveta Peschke combination and I was a bit apprehensive about our quarter-final duel. Happily, I struck a purple patch and played one of my best matches ever. My returns against Mike Bryan's serve were spot on and seemed to take the master doubles player by surprise on several occasions. Mahesh took care of Peschke at the net and we marched confidently into the semi-finals with an authoritative 6-2, 6-3 win without even breaking into a sweat.

We then overwhelmed the Kazakh–Italian duo of Galina Voskoboeva and Daniele Bracciali 6-2, 6-1. I sealed the win with a crushing backhand winner on our first match point. We had now reached our third Grand Slam final together and awaited the winner of the Leander Paes–Elena Vesnina and Santiago Gonzalez–Klaudia Jans semi-final. There was a strong possibility that three Indians would be figuring in the battle for the French Open title. The Indo-Russian team was in the fight all through the first set before Santiago Gonzalez and Klaudia Jans took it in the tie-breaker and then won the second set comfortably to book a showdown with us in the summit clash. This was to be their first Grand Slam final and we thought our experience would give us the advantage.

The final was delayed due to inclement weather and the tournament director was considering shifting it out of Philippe Chatrier Court but Mahesh wouldn't hear of it. Playing a Grand Slam final involves overcoming nerves and the wily Mahesh knew that we stood to gain by playing on the daunting centre court against the inexperienced Mexican-Polish pair, who were competing in the first really big match of their career.

The final began in overcast conditions after some delay and initially, I found myself struggling in the tense atmosphere. I was glad to have Hesh, buddy and battle-scarred veteran, on my side of the net to calm my nerves. We missed the opportunity to break Gonzalez in the first game and then I lost my serve as we went down 1-3. We drew parity in the tenth game on the Mexican's serve and won the tie-breaker with some sparkling tennis. I was now beginning to find my feet and rhythm and Mahesh was peaking as well.

The second set was a no-contest as we breezed through with absolute ease for our second Grand Slam title together. 'We play a dangerous kind of tennis. When we are playing our best, it's kind of hard to beat us,' Mahesh said with a twinkle in his eye at the post-match ceremony on court. It was his thirty-eighth birthday and when it was my turn to speak, I said, 'Now I don't have to think of a gift to give my partner!'

The thrill of winning a Grand Slam title at Roland Garros was adequate compensation for the disappointment I had felt a year ago when Vesnina and I went down in the final of the women's doubles. I had been on the losing side in a final at the French Open in 2011 and exactly a year later I had bagged the prestigious trophy, albeit in a different category.

We went out for dinner to celebrate, to an Indian restaurant at the foot of the Eiffel Tower. After all, this was a very special day. I was now a two-time Grand Slam winner and had just won a title with a fellow Indian at Roland Garros on clay – a surface that my critics had always believed I was incapable of performing on. The win would also seal my spot with Mahesh in the mixed doubles draw of the Olympics once my wild card was assured by ITF, and that was now a mere formality. We had shown the world the magic that Hesh and I could produce as a team and an Olympic medal in tennis for India seemed a real possibility a few weeks from now, in London.

33

THE LONDON DRAMA

A FEW WEEKS before the lighting of the historic flame for the 2012 London Olympics, all the talk in the Indian media centred on who was to partner whom in the men's doubles draw. I preferred to focus on mixed doubles, the event that I had a chance to play and win a medal in.

Securing my spot at the Games was a daunting task in the first place. According to the rules, I needed to be in the women's doubles draw in order to be eligible to participate in the mixed, in which lay my best chance for a medal. With my high ranking, getting into the women's doubles would have been a done deal, but only if we had another Indian around the top-100 mark on the cut-off date of 11 June 2012. Unfortunately, we had no other female tennis player ranked even in the top-300.

There was just one option: I would have to secure my spot inside the top-10 in doubles. That would allow me to play the women's doubles draw in London with any Indian partner of my choice, no matter how low her ranking. It would also get me into the mixed doubles draw and that was a definite priority.

I'd had a phenomenal year, making it to the semi-finals with Ves in the Australian Open and finishing as runners-up in Dubai and Indian Wells, where we played our second consecutive final together. I had also won the Pattaya Open with Anastasia Rodionova and the

Brussels Open doubles title with Bethanie Mattek-Sands. That had brought me to No. 10 in the world but I needed another big effort in the women's draw of Roland Garros to seal my Olympic spot.

I had been the runner-up the previous year in the French Open doubles and needed to defend those points in order to ensure my entry into the Olympics. According to my calculations, I would have to reach the quarter-finals at Roland Garros.

My partner Bethanie and I had won in Brussels the previous week and our morale was high. Unfortunately Beth injured her toe while playing in the singles a day before our doubles event and we were unable to perform to our potential, bowing out of the Grand Slam in the first round itself against the unfancied pair of Edina Gallovits-Hall and Nina Bratchikova in three tough sets. As a result, I finished at No. 11 on the cut-off date of 11 June – tantalizingly close and yet not quite there. Of course, there was still some hope of being awarded a wild-card entry, which I thought Hesh and I deserved.

While I was totally engrossed in my bid to qualify for the London Olympics, plenty was happening amongst the big boys of Indian tennis as the race to seal their spots with a partner of their choice heated up. Hesh and Rohan had been partnering together on the tour and, for obvious reasons, wanted to play as a team. Leander, on the other hand, was the top-ranked Indian and felt he deserved to pick the partner who would give him the best chance. The plotting and politicking were now being played out in public with AITA throwing its weight behind Leander and appearing to give him the option to play with a partner of his choice. The media was having a field day thanks to this self-induced chaos but it was the prestige of Indian tennis that was suffering cruelly.

I preferred to stay out of the massive controversy that had broken out as I honestly believed it had nothing to do with me. I was asked many times for my opinion, but I thought it was none of my business to speak publicly on an issue that did not concern me. I was not even a part of the Olympic team yet.

If I was awarded the wild card, I would be delighted to play with

Rushmi Chakravarthi, whose name AITA had proposed as my partner for the Olympics in recognition of her being the No. 2 player of India. In mixed doubles, I assumed Mahesh and I would be the automatic choice for several reasons. We had not only won two Grand Slam titles together – one of them only a few weeks ago at Roland Garros – but had also reached the semi-finals at the previous Grand Slam in January in Melbourne. Besides, Mahesh is an ad court specialist and complements me perfectly as I prefer the deuce court that suits the forehand, my biggest strength.

While Mahesh and I were busy playing the French Open and making our way through a difficult draw en route to our title win, AITA president Anil Khanna had come to meet us. Before our quarter-final, he spoke to Leander and Mahesh separately. I don't know what he said to the others, but he told me after my match that I could play with whoever I wanted to, in the mixed doubles at the Olympics. I think at that point everyone was aware that Mahesh and I were expecting to play together. Khanna stayed over and watched our next match too, where we beat the top seeds. It was a particularly good show from me in the match. After the win, he told Dad, 'The way Sania is playing, she can win with anyone.' Maybe he could feel the Olympic storm brewing and was hinting at the eventuality of me not getting to play with my desired partner.

In a shocking move, my name was dragged in as a compromise formula to end the deadlock among the male doubles players. AITA announced that I would partner Leander Paes in the mixed doubles in an obvious effort to end the feud among the men. In effect, they sacrificed India's best chance of winning an Olympic medal in tennis by breaking up a proven winning combination. I was absolutely livid.

I had never felt more angry or let down as I did when the provisional team for the Olympics was announced. Mahesh and Rohan were allowed to play together and Leander was paired with Vishnu Vardhan. In the process, it was I who was sacrificed. Yet, I did not wish to jump the gun and speak out until my wild card was confirmed by ITF. It made little sense to go public when I was not even certain of playing at the London Games.

I had just won my first-round match at Wimbledon when ITF confirmed my wild-card entry into the women's doubles event with Rushmi as my partner. I was now officially a part of the 2012 Olympics and I decided that it was the right time to make my stand clear on a few burning issues that had dogged me for the last few days. I consulted my father in the Players' Lounge about speaking to the media and letting them know how I felt about the way I was being treated.

I then picked up a pen and paper in the locker room and feverishly wrote out a press release. I had stayed out of the controversy for as long as I possibly could, but now that they had collectively dragged me in, I felt the need to straighten things out and let my heart do the talking. This is what I said in my statement:

I feel absolutely thrilled and emotionally overwhelmed to have qualified to represent India at the Olympics in London. I am extremely grateful to the International Tennis Federation for the faith they have reposed in me by giving me a wild-card entry that offers me a cherished opportunity to represent my country at the Olympics for the second time in my life.

While, of course, nobody in the world can guarantee winning a medal in London, I can promise that I shall leave no stone unturned to bring glory to my beloved country.

I have to admit that helplessly watching the sport that I love and passionately play, go through extremely trying times in my country in the last few days and the unusual pressures that I was personally subjected to have left me shaken and disturbed. But I can assure all my countrymen that I shall never allow these difficult circumstances to come in the way of giving my very best when the Games begin.

Since the day AITA announced the team for the Olympics a lot of questions have been raised by friends, colleagues, their parents and of course, by the media. As I thought these questions were purely hypothetical without my having qualified into the London Olympics, I did not think it was appropriate for me to respond to them at that point of time. However, now that I am officially a part of the greatest sporting event in the world, I think it is imperative for me to clarify my feelings.

To Dr Vece Paes, who has on camera, asked me to give in writing about my intention of partnering his son for the mixed doubles event at the Olympics, I would like to point out that my commitment is to my country. For the sake of India I am committed to play with Leander Paes or Mahesh Bhupathi or Rohan Bopanna or Somdev Devvarman or Vishnu Vardhan or any other person that my country feels I am good enough to partner. There should never ever be a question on this although if asked, I am entitled to have my preferences. I will do everything I possibly can to win a medal for India.

To Leander Paes I would like to point out that Vishnu Vardhan is an extremely talented player, who I had the privilege of partnering. We went on to win a silver medal for India at the 2010 Asian Games, when all the three male stalwarts of Indian tennis had opted to stay away from Guangzhou. I am convinced that he can go one better when pitted with someone as good as Leander as partner. For Leander to consider partnering with Vishnu only if he has a written assurance from me to play mixed (as Vece Uncle has suggested in his television interviews) is, I think demeaning for me, Vishnu and Leander Paes.

Mahesh Bhupathi has firmly stood by his commitment to play together with his men's doubles partner, Rohan Bopanna as he genuinely believed it was good for India. However, in the process, he sacrificed the commitment he made to me to try and win an Olympic medal together for India. Each person has his or her own priorities and I would like to believe that Mahesh made his choice in the best interests of the country.

As an Indian woman belonging to the 21st century, what I find disillusioning is the humiliating manner in which I was put up as a bait to try and pacify one of the disgruntled stalwarts of Indian tennis. While I feel honoured and privileged to have *been chosen to partner Leander Paes, the manner and timing of the announcement reeks of male chauvinism where a two time Grand Slam champion, who has been India's No. 1 women's tennis player for almost a decade in singles and doubles is offered in compensation to partner one of the feuding champions purely in order to lure him into accepting to play with a men's player he does not wish to play with! This kind of blatant humiliation of Indian womanhood needs to be condemned even if it comes from the highest controlling body of tennis in our country.*

I have been fortunate to achieve a career best singles ranking of 27 in the world that has been only bettered by Vijay Amritraj (16) and Ramesh Krishnan (23) even amongst the men in the modern era. I have a career-best doubles ranking of 7 in the world, which only Leander Paes and Mahesh Bhupathi have bettered. I am the only Grand Slam champion from India apart from Mahesh and Leander. I believe I can expect a little more respect from the National Tennis Federation than what has been accorded to me even if they did not think it necessary to send me a simple congratulatory message after I had won my second Grand Slam title three weeks ago.

What is even more shocking is the manner in which facts have been misrepresented to the public at large to paint a totally wrong picture in an attempt to justify the breaking up of a team that won a second Grand Slam title only days earlier. Leander and I are not the only combination likely to get a direct entry into the mixed doubles draw at the Olympics, as has been wrongly portrayed. If that was true, a highly intelligent man like Dr Paes would not have felt insecure enough to ask for my written declaration to partner Leander. AITA itself would not have needed to write a letter to Mr Randhir Singh giving details of the final pairings and clarifying that these could not be changed without the written permission of the IOA!

I would like to reiterate that I consider it the ultimate honour to represent India to the best of my abilities at the Olympics and I

*will do everything I possibly can with whosoever I am partnered
with. This has always been my stand and this will never change.
I only seek the blessings of the people of our beloved country.
Nothing more!*

After having sent out the press statement, I felt exhausted and
emotionally drained. Within minutes, my cellphone began to ring.
The media wanted me to elaborate on what I had said. But there was
nothing left for me to say. I switched my phone off and cried bitterly
in a corner of the Wimbledon locker room.

My press statement had a big impact back home and the feuding
parties were stunned into silence. There was massive support in the
media for what I had said and women's organizations were up in
arms, though that was not what I was looking for. I had been pushed
to the wall and I felt I owed it to myself to speak up against what I
sincerely believed were deeply unfortunate circumstances. My stance
also hit a chord with many other women athletes, who had suffered
disrespect in their chosen fields. Many had raised their voices against
such chauvinism, but with little impact. I received an outpouring of
support from them.

While everyone had a view on what I had said, the article that
really touched me was written by my senior colleague, Nirupama
Vaidyanathan (now Nirupama Sanjeev), the former India No. 1. In a
piece charged with emotion, Niru wrote:

*Male chauvinism was something I lived with, it was part of our
culture. There was an underlying sneer and nonchalance about
women and sports in India. While my immediate family and
friends in the town of Coimbatore were quite supportive of my
endeavour, there were a few who knew how to put a dampener
on things. They would try to advise my dad into saying: 'She
is somebody else's "property". Why are you spending so much
money on her?' We lived with this sort of thing every day. But
this was more than fifteen years ago, years before Sania Mirza
came blazing onto the scene.*

This is now. Sania Mirza is made to face the brunt of male chauvinism when she was literally made a pawn to appease Leander Paes. Sania's statement after her wild card was announced could not have been more emphatic. No player of India should have been used as a pawn in egotistical dramas. She is, after all, the undisputed queen of Indian tennis and the ONLY player, male or female, who can actually fill a 5,000-capacity stadium in India. Her diplomacy and single-minded intent of putting India first are traits that our men may have forgotten. The timing of this statement was impeccable and so was the content.

I can only sympathize with her and hope she can put all this behind her when she starts her campaign in London. Knowing the woman she is, these things are bound to make her stronger mentally as she has a way of coming through against all odds.

It had taken an experienced female tennis player from my own country to fully comprehend how cornered and claustrophobic I had felt during those dark days. Niru's understanding words provided solace to me at a time when I was more disturbed than I had ever been.

The 2012 Olympics had certainly not had the right kind of build-up, but as professionals, when we finally made it to London for the Games, every one of us wanted nothing less than to win for our country. Leander and I tried our best and I am certain that was the case with Mahesh and Rohan too. It is unfortunate that a medal eluded us but there is also no denying that I will continue to feel I was robbed of a genuine chance to win a mixed doubles medal at the 2012 Games. This is not to suggest that Leander and I had no chance at all to win. But the Bhupathi–Mirza combination would definitely have had a better shot, especially at a time when we were combining so well together and had won the French Open just weeks earlier. I believe I was shortchanged and so was my beloved country.

34

THE DOUBLES MISSION

THERE WAS A phase in my career when I struggled to find the right doubles partner for myself. With the approach of the London Olympics, Elena Vesnina decided to play on tour with her country mate Ekaterina Makarova, to prepare for the big event. This turned out to be a blessing in disguise. Though Elena and I had done extremely well, we had not won many tournaments together and a Grand Slam title still eluded us. Maybe there was something missing in our chemistry.

I had decided to partner Bethanie Mattek-Sands on a permanent basis but she was injured and out of action for the first few weeks, so I played in Portugal with Anastasia Rodionova. We had won the Pattaya Open together, at the start of the year. Roddy and I reached the semi-finals in Portugal but the following week Bethanie and I started off in the Brussels tournament, which we won. I thought we combined beautifully, as we had always done, but a week later, Bethanie injured herself during her singles match at Roland Garros and that's when the bad streak began.

We lost in the first round of Roland Garros with Bethanie struggling in pain. It was disappointing to finally have a partner who seemed to be combining so well with me and then to have her struck down with injury. Beth needed treatment and would now only come back for Wimbledon after a period of rest. So I was forced to play with whoever I could find in the run-up to the grass court Slam.

I partnered Yaroslava Shvedova in Birmingham just after she had a very good run in singles at the French Open. Perhaps she was not quite ready to focus on doubles after the staggering singles performance on clay the week before and we lost in the first round. In Eastbourne, I partnered former world No. 1 Paola Suarez and as luck would have it, the South American injured herself even before the tournament began. She tried gamely to play the first round, but retired after the opening set. This was an extremely tough period for me because I had to find partners at short notice, scratch combines here and there, and even those players were getting hurt.

I felt I deserved to win more often than I was doing. I went into Wimbledon with no wins on grass and with a partner who was coming back to the game after a lay-off. Yet, Bethanie and I won a couple of matches before running into the rampaging Williams sisters in the third round, in which I was cheered on by actress and good friend Raveena Tandon and her family, who had come down to watch me play.

After the Olympics, we went to Montreal for the Rogers Cup and scored a couple of good wins – beating seventh seeds Julia Goerges–Kveta Peschke in the first round and Dominika Cibulkova–Daniela Hantuchova in the second. But we went down in the quarter-finals to third seeds Nadia Petrova and Katarina Srebotnik in the super tie-breaker. We lost the decider 8-10 in the first round in Cincinnati as well, this time to Ekaterina Makarova–Anna Tatishvili.

I approached the US Open with just two wins under my belt – another Grand Slam with barely the right build-up. This was really not turning out to be the kind of year I'd been hoping to have since the change of partners. We scored two good victories in Flushing Meadows but then ran into second seeds Sara Errani and Roberta Vinci, who were the upcoming doubles combination and fast developing into a top team. We lost 7-9 in a tough second set tie-break after winning the opener 6-4. It was the first time we had lost a set so far in the tournament. That broke our back and we went down 3-6 in the third set. Not surprisingly, the Italian duo went on to win the championships – they were clearly the new team to beat on the tour.

Bethanie was injured again and skipped the Asian leg post the US Open. We were really good together and believed we could beat any team on the women's tour but the regular injury breaks never gave us a chance to reach our potential. I was left high and dry in Asia, trying to survive while once again looking for any partner who was available.

I played with Anabel Medina Garrigues in Seoul and lost a tough match in the super tie-break in the first round. I then partnered Nuria Llagostera Vives for Tokyo, Beijing and Moscow. After losing in the first round in Japan in yet another super tie-break, we turned it around in Beijing, making it to the final. We lost to Vesnina and Makarova in the battle for the title. I was yearning for the No. 1 spot in the world, I knew I was good enough to achieve it, but was having a nightmare of a year despite my game being as good as it had ever been. I lost in the quarters in Moscow, my last event for 2012, and finished the year at an individual ranking of 12 in doubles. This was deeply frustrating, for I knew I could do better.

*

Despite Bethanie's uncertain physical condition, we decided to play together in 2013 as well. The undeniable fact was that a fit Bethanie and I were the best team on the tour. The run of bad luck with her injuries would have to change at some point. There was no reason to stop – we had delivered in the past and were the best of friends. We justified this decision by coming back and winning the first title of 2013 at Brisbane. It was an endorsement of how good we were despite the lack of regular matches and the ease with which we won the title reinforced our faith in the partnership.

Due to her lay-off, Bethanie's ranking had dropped considerably and she needed to play the qualifying rounds for the upcoming Australian Open. Singles was still her prime focus and I once again needed to look for a partner for the one event in between Brisbane and Melbourne. I came together with former world No. 1 Liezel Huber in Sydney and lost in the quarters. Going into the first Grand Slam of the year, I still felt Bethanie and I could do well. After all, we had just won a title together. Unfortunately, Bethanie's health problems continued. She came into the match with yet another injury, something to do with her hip, and made a brave attempt, but struggled all through the match. Not surprisingly, we lost in straight sets. We had to skip yet another event following the Grand Slam and when we reunited in Doha, we lost in the first round.

Since giving up singles, doubles was all I had, but the rub of the green was just not going my way. It was in these circumstances that Bethanie and I beat some of the best teams in the world to win in Dubai, much against the run of play in that period. We won 10-7 in the super tie-break against second seeds Nadia Petrova and Katarina Srebotnik in the final. Football legend Diego Maradona was amongst those watching the match and he came down to the court to meet us after the final. It was a brief but pleasant meeting with the legend and we posed for a lot of pictures.

After a first round exit in Indian Wells and the quarter-finals in Miami, where we lost to top seeds Sara Errani–Roberta Vinci, we bounced back strongly to make the final in Stuttgart again, but our seeding suffered because of our staccato run. We had a poor showing in Madrid and lost the quarter-finals in Rome to Errani-Vinci, the then No. 1 team in the world and our new nemesis. But any momentum we had managed to gain as a team was lost once more as Bethanie had to play the qualifying rounds for the singles of the French Open. Since the dates coincided, we could not defend our title in Brussels from the previous year. I had to play with Jie Zheng, my seventh partner since splitting with Vesnina.

We won the first round at Roland Garros but Bethanie was injured again while playing singles. Against the rank outsiders, Americans Lauren Davis and Megan Moulton-Levy, we lost the first set 1-6 with Bethanie hardly able to move. We were on the brink of being humiliated and I was losing patience. Bethanie somehow turned it around by pushing herself mentally and we won 6-3, 6-0 in the next two sets although I was unsure if my partner would be able to play on in the tournament. We had managed to step it up just in time against the unranked Americans, but up next were eleventh seeds Anastasia Pavlyuchenkova from Russia and Lucie Safarova of the Czech Republic. We won a tight first set 7-6 after outplaying them in the tie-break but Beth's injury had worsened. We struggled our way to 3-5 down in the second set, at which point her pain became unmanageable and we had to throw in the towel as she retired. She had hurt her adductor muscle and was in extreme pain.

It was becoming excruciatingly painful for me to carry on like this. I was hungry for big titles, but for more than a year and five Slams now, my results had been ordinary. Patches of brilliance were not enough to satisfy me. I needed solidity and stability. I wanted to be the No. 1 player in the world!

Bethanie is one of my dearest friends and she herself knew this was no way to carry on. Finally, at the end of the French Open, she told me she loved playing with me but her body was letting her down. She asked me to look for a new partner. The tear in her adductor muscle meant she would struggle on the grass court and she was clear her body was not going to be able to take the load of singles and doubles together for a long time. The two of us get along like a house on fire and have continued to remain the best of friends, but I had no time to lose. Wimbledon was round the corner.

My old mentor, Liezel Huber, was looking for a partner and we decided to combine again. She was nowhere close to her peak but the situation was getting desperate for me. After losing in the quarter-finals in Eastbourne, we lost the third round at Wimbledon against the unfancied Shuko Aoyama and Chanelle Scheepers. The modest success with Liezel meant that I now needed to look for a new partner again in the run-up to the US hard court season.

I played one tournament with Flavia Penetta and then came back with Jie Zheng, with whom I had poor results in Toronto and Cincinnati but a surprise title win in New Haven. It took Zheng and me some time to build a rapport. We lost to two teams we should have never lost to, but we had made a commitment to each other. In the first round in New Haven, we were playing the same duo we had lost to in Toronto – Oksana Kalashnikova and Alicja Rosolska. We were on the verge of losing again when, at 8-8 in the super tie-breaker, our opponents missed an easy overhead. Nine times out of ten, this would be a simple put away shot but Rosolska shanked it out of the court. We ended up winning the match and the momentum shifted in our favour from there on.

In the quarter-final against Katalin Marosi and Megan Moulton-Levy, we were down 2-5 in the super tie-break. Zheng was at the net and my forehand from the back of the court hit her on the head as she stood up unexpectedly. The ball smacked her hard enough to bounce back over the baseline behind us. We were now down 2-6, but somehow came around to win the match. We never looked back and probably went on to play some of our best tennis to pocket the match. Jie Zheng's affable husband was in high spirits after the win and jokingly said to me that every time his wife was not playing well, all I needed to do was hit her on the head with the ball since it seemed to do wonders for her game!

We went on to win the title by beating second seeds Anabel Medina Garrigues and Katarina Srebotnik in the final. We had started playing as a team. I could sense that every time a partner gave me enough support, it was resulting in a title win. If only I could find someone to stand by me on a regular basis on court, the doubles world could be conquered.

We went on to reach the semis of the US Open, losing to eighth-seeded Aussies Ashleigh Barty and Casey Dellacqua. It was just not our day. Jie Zheng was not at her best, and she told me after the loss that she felt she had let me down. Earlier, after our losses in the first two events, I had touched base with former World No. 1 Cara Black. However, since my partnership with Jie Zheng had begun to click, I was no longer sure about the right course to follow. Eventually, it was scheduling issues that made us split up. Jie Zheng did not want to play the upcoming event in Beijing after Tokyo. That was where I was defending a bunch of points from a final appearance in 2012.

Cara, though, was available for both or none. So the choice became simple. Instead of playing two events with two different players or not playing Beijing at all, I decided to split with Jie Zheng and team up with Cara. We would see how we fared together before thinking about a future partnership.

That was where the turnaround began. The streak of bad luck was finally done with.

Cara and I scorched the courts of Tokyo and Beijing to pocket both titles with a scintillating display. In the first round in Tokyo, we lost the opening set even before we had adjusted to each other's game. Cara relies almost entirely on her reflexes and volleys at the net and it took us a while to understand each other's strengths. We beat the top seeds, Su-Wei Hsieh and Peng Shuai, in Tokyo in the semi-final, on our way to the title. We even saved a couple of match points at 7-9 in the super tie-break in the final, against Hao-Ching Chan and Liezel Huber. Perhaps this was the moment when I began to believe that we had struck up a key partnership. We went from strength to strength. In Beijing we did not lose a set and in the semis, we went one up on the team of Errani-Vinci that had proved to be almost unbeatable in the past.

With two big title wins, 2013 came to a brilliant end. I had won five titles in the year from six finals with three partners, but it was the end of the year that carried a lot of hope for the future. My only regret was that despite winning a WTA tour high of five titles in 2013, I could not qualify for the prestigious year-end championships as the wins had been accomplished with different partners. I finished the year at an individual doubles ranking of No. 9. I had missed the cut for the year-end event in which only the best eight teams qualified but felt encouraged by the fact that I had made my way back into the top-10 again.

35

A MIXED SEASON

Soon after the Beijing win, Cara and I decided to play together and I spoke to Jie Zheng to let her know that it made more sense for me to continue with my new partner. 'I think you will do better with her,' she agreed, sportingly.

Cara came over to Hyderabad for the off-season training. We knew we had a lot of work to do as the competition would be gunning for us. Videos of our wins would have been circulated and teams would have devised ways to counter us. I had worked in the past on the tour with Australian trainer Robert Ballard and invited him to Hyderabad to prepare us for the next season. Robert's credentials were impeccable. A former Olympic athlete, he had rubbed shoulders with the likes of Carl Lewis and Ben Johnson. As a trainer, he had worked with the Indonesian Davis Cup team and also travelled on the WTA and ATP tours. Robert was extremely innovative and had a scientific approach to training. He had benchmarks for the top athletes in the world and measured your level through comparison charts that he formulated. He made us push cars and lift tractor tyres among other things!

Christian Filhol, the French coach who had worked with Cara for a long time, joined us in Hyderabad at the Sania Mirza Tennis Academy, which had finally been inaugurated a few months earlier after years of struggle. It had been the Mirza family's dream to set up an international level tennis centre in our country that could provide all the world-class facilities that I had missed out on while developing as a youngster, and the sheer thrill of watching our dreams take concrete shape was immensely satisfying. The top players of the country, men and women, were also over at the academy for a camp, making it a few intensive weeks of hard work and fun.

The start of the year 2014 was not great. We just did not get into the match on a windy day, losing in the first round in Sydney against Australian imports Jarmila Gajdosova and Ajla Tomljanovic, two singles players who can play a handy brand of doubles. They possess considerable power in their ground strokes and can serve big as well. We wanted to quickly get over this loss and reach into our confidence from the previous season as we headed into the Australian Open. We were looking good and had not lost a set when we came up against Sara Errani and Roberta Vinci again, in the quarters.

We won the first set, lost the second, and were two breaks up in the third at 4-1 with me serving. That is when the tables turned and everything that the Italians tried seemed to work. Obviously, Cara and I still had some loose ends between us, which we needed to work on. There appeared to be a lack of fine-tuning and this hurt us as we lost from a very strong position and the top seeds went on to win the title. It was not a bad showing from us – quarters in our first Slam together – but we seemed to have slipped up. At the back of my mind, this was another missed opportunity. If we had clinched this win, we would have had a very good chance of winning the title, and the No. 1 spot would have been much closer.

In the next few weeks it became clearer to us that we still had work to do as we lost some very tight matches in Doha and Dubai. Our morale was taking a hit too, with the start of the year being nowhere close to what I had envisaged after the two titles towards the end of 2013.

Indian Wells was next on the schedule. I always looked forward to playing at this picturesque venue. The conditions suit me – the ball travels a little bit faster and although it's more difficult to control, it adds some nip to my ground strokes. Also, importantly, I have a lot of friends and family in the area, and they come to watch me play every year. Aunt Anjum and her husband Junaid drive up almost every day. There is home-cooked food which my aunt packs and brings. It has become customary for us to drive down to their home in San Diego to spend some time and unwind in case we lose earlier than in the final. It was my aunt who sent me my first quality tennis racket from USA when I was six years old and taking baby steps in the game that was to become my life.

I settled my record against Vesnina and Makarova in the quarter-final with a fluent straight-set win. However, we lost the final to the better team on the day, Su-Wei Hsieh and Peng Shuai. The former was in particularly good form at this time, which was why I opted for her as a partner later. Meanwhile, the problems Cara and I had encountered with the overhead shot, which was a significant chink in our armour at the start of the year, had been settled. The thumb rule was that Cara would handle these. She rarely missed the stroke and that added to our strength.

We made the semis in Miami next, after winning a fiercely fought first round 10-8 in the super tie-breaker against the Chan sisters. In the end we were beaten by Martina Hingis and Sabine Lisicki, with the former World No. 1 making a return to doubles and going on to win the title. But Cara and I had got back on track now and I had started to believe again that we could be world-beaters. There was still one big hurdle, though, in the form of the Italian duo. In the final at Stuttgart, we lost yet again to the top team in the world, Errani–Vinci. They had us figured out completely and we didn't seem to have the weapons to beat them, especially on clay.

Meanwhile, our performance kept getting better as we won the Estoril Open in Portugal, beating the experienced team of former World No. 1s, Lisa Raymond and Liezel Huber, in the semis. This was one of the best matches I had played in a long time. I was striking the ball with great finesse. I had always liked playing doubles on clay as it gave me more time to set up the stroke. The serve-and-volley players found it harder to control my ball at the net as I got more time to unleash my power.

In the quarter-finals in Madrid, we lost again to Hsieh and Peng, who had now taken over as the No. 1 team in the world. It was anybody's match and could have gone either way. Hsieh impressed me again with her game, especially her unorthodox brilliance at the net. Her reflexes were unbelievable and she had the flair of a magician.

In Rome, we avenged our earlier loss against Hingis and Lisicki but were again stopped in our tracks by Errani and Vinci. At Roland Garros we were beaten by Hsieh and Peng for the third time that year and it became only too evident that we needed to quickly find a solution to the Chinese and Italian teams if we were to dominate women's doubles. We seemed to be doing well except in the Slams and this was a worry for me, given my burning ambition to become the best doubles player in the world.

We went into the grass court season with high expectations, as this was a surface that suited Cara well. She had the reflexes and volleys which could make the difference. My sister Anam joined me and my father for a few weeks. Shoaib was playing cricket for Warwickshire in Birmingham while we were in the same city for my tournament and we all stayed together in an apartment. It was fun as we watched each other's matches, and even some movies, and shopped endlessly with Cara and her husband 'Moose'.

Shoaib was having a great run on the cricket field in his T20 tournament, playing for the English county, but the results on court for me were not as good as we had anticipated. We suffered two bad losses, going down after being way ahead in the super tie-breakers – in the semi-final in Birmingham and the quarter-final in Eastbourne.

Despite these setbacks, we felt confident going into Wimbledon. Cara had a superb record at Wimbledon and I loved the grass at the Big 'W' as well. We scored a straightforward first-round win but nothing could have prepared us for what followed next. We missed nine match points in the second round against Anastasia Pavlyuchenkova and Lucie Safarova in the most heartbreaking loss of my career. We didn't do anything wrong but the opponents produced some mind-boggling tennis, hitting aces and winners to the lines on demand.

I went back to the apartment after the match and did not speak to anyone. I remember Shoaib calling to me to come out of the room but I just wanted the day to be over. I must have woken up half a dozen times during the night, often after reliving the nightmare of the missed match points. Finally I got out of bed at 8 a.m., still in a daze from the strange loss.

Even though families of athletes understand what they go through on a daily basis, there are times when it's impossible even for those close to them to really know the extent of the pain. I just did not want to talk to anybody. When Shoaib tried to make conversation in an attempt to take my mind off the loss, I lashed out at him. Though an athlete himself, I did not think it was possible for him to fully understand what I was going through. Such moments are incredibly hard on everyone as you end up snapping at the very people you love the most.

I knew I was being difficult and emotional but I did not even want to see the tennis court the next morning. It took me several days to get over the painful loss. I felt despondent and anxious, wondering if my plans were ever going to work out. My goals were still some distance away and though I was playing at a very high level, I knew that my form would not last forever.

Soon after I got back to Hyderabad from Wimbledon, I became embroiled in another unnecessary controversy. The chief minister of my newly formed state, Chandrasekhar Rao, graciously appointed me as the brand ambassador of Telangana. Of course, it was a great honour for me and I accepted the appointment with humility. A couple of politicians saw an opportunity to create a controversy and issued public statements questioning my credentials – as an Indian, a Hyderabadi, and finally as the brand ambassador of Telangana. Their attempts to create trouble, perhaps with the intention of politically milking a non-issue, failed miserably as quite significantly their own party men silenced them with strong words.

Initially, when this new controversy broke out, I felt disturbed but soon gathered myself.

'It hurts me that so much precious time of prominent politicians and the media is being wasted on the issue of my being appointed the brand ambassador of my state of Telangana. I sincerely believe that this precious time should be spent on solving the more urgent issues of our state and country,' I said in a press release to clarify my position on the subject.

'I was born in Mumbai as my mother needed to be at a specialist hospital since she was seriously unwell at the time of my birth. I came home to Hyderabad when I was three weeks old. My forefathers have lived in Hyderabad for more than a century. I'm an Indian who will remain an Indian until the end of my life. My family has belonged to Hyderabad for more than a century and I strongly condemn any attempts by any person to brand me an outsider.'

The media rallied around with massive support for me and I felt grateful for this. The controversy died a sudden death and soon I could focus again on the upcoming tournaments. Being appointed the brand ambassador of Telangana seemed to turn my luck around. My performances and career gathered momentum as I went on to win four Grand Slam titles, two medals in the Asian Games, two year-end WTA championships and eleven World Ranking tour titles.

With the latest controversy done and dusted, I moved into the US hard court season. Anam travelled with me this time, chipping in as my manager in the absence of my father, who joined us a few weeks later, before the US Open. Anam's close friend, Tanya, a former national-level junior tennis player who trains at my academy in Hyderabad, accompanied us too.

After a bad start in Washington, we earned back some confidence in Montreal, making it to the final. We beat the Chinese pair of Hsieh and Peng 13-11 in the tie-breaker, for our first win in the last four matches that we had played against them in 2014. Before they hit their stride and reached the top spot, I had held a head-to-head record of 4-0 against the Chinese while playing with different partners. Disappointingly, we lost again in the final in straight sets to Errani–Vinci, who were back to being the No. 1 team.

We had rather ordinary tournaments in Cincinnati and New Haven and came to the last Slam of the year, a little concerned that we had not quite delivered yet. We desperately needed to strike it rich here. Remarkably, we were handed the same draw in the first two rounds of the US Open as at the previous event in New Haven. We defeated identical twins Karolina and Kristyna Pliskova in the first round and then met Caroline Garcia and Monica Niculescu again in the second, this time beating them comfortably in straight sets. We seemed to be striking form at just the right time.

We continued to play strong tennis and reached the last-four stage without losing a set. We now faced Martina Hingis and Flavia Pennetta for a place in the final. We fancied our chances but were completely outplayed by the scratch pair – a disappointing end to a good tournament. However, under the circumstances, we were happy to have made the semis, even though, as a team, it was clear that we were not winning enough titles.

*

Post my French Open mixed doubles title in 2012 with Mahesh Bhupathi, I had played alongside Britain's Colin Fleming in the US Open and had an extended run with Romanian Horia Tecau, starting with Wimbledon 2013. We continued to play together in five consecutive Grand Slams till Wimbledon 2014. I had been impressed with Horia ever since Mahesh and I first played him and Bethanie in the Australian Open. We had ended up on the losing side in 2012 and Mattek–Tecau had gone on to win the title after beating Leander and Vesnina in the final. While most people took it for granted that I would continue playing with Hesh, the heartbreaking episode before the London Olympics had strained our professional relationship and I felt the need to move on.

Horia and I had some decent results, but we did not win a Grand Slam. Our best performance came at the 2014 Australian Open, where we lost in the final to 'Kiki' Mladenovic and Daniel

Nestor. We were completely outplayed after having a good run till the final.

We split in the summer after playing the French Open and Wimbledon that year as I felt I had the potential to not just do well but to win a few more Grand Slam titles before I was through with my career. Hesh's ex-coach Scott Davidoff, a good friend who had worked with me during an off-season in India, was coaching Brazilian Bruno Soares at the time and became the catalyst for our pairing up at the US Open 2014.

While he did not have Tecau's powerful serve, Bruno's game was very similar to Mahesh's and that was a definite positive that worked well for our new combination. He had brilliant hands at the net and his returns were reliable, complementing my own natural strengths. We struggled initially against a wild-card pair in the first round but scraped through in the super tie-breaker.

I played an outstanding match in the quarter-final against compatriot Rohan Bopanna and his partner. In the super tie-break, I worked up some magic that turned the match, which had been on an even keel till then, completely in our favour. We made the finals where we faced Santiago Gonzalez and Abigail Spears.

Hesh and I had beaten Gonzalez in the final of the French Open in 2012, albeit with a different partner. I knew exactly how he played. He struggled to generate speed on the backhand when not given pace and serving at a reduced speed onto his weaker side was an effective weapon. The tactic worked and we won the first set easily at 6-1. Gonzalez–Spears came back to take the second 6-2 with Bruno's serve dipping a bit.

The super tie-breaker seemed to be going in our favour as we worked up a commanding 9-4 lead but just when it all seemed over, nerves got the better of us. Spears and Gonzalez brought it back to 9-all. At 9-8 Bruno served to Abigail and came in. He had the ball on his racket but in a moment of complete madness he let it go and it landed a good two feet in.

Now the US Open title hinged on stringing two good points back-to-back and we happened to be the team that did it. As Bruno served to Gonzalez at match point, we had a brilliant exchange of strokes with Abigail and Gonzales charging at the net, and under extreme pressure, with a Grand Slam title at stake, we held our nerve to win the championship.

Expectations are always low from mixed doubles because it is never easy to predict anything in this format. So winning this title in our very first Slam together was a source of immense jubilation. My father and sister and Bruno's wife and mother-in-law joined in the celebrations, though we did not have much time as I was already booked to come back to India before going to Tokyo and preparing for the Asian Games.

The Grand Slam win turned out to be rather bittersweet because I entered the locker after the final to find my doubles partner, Cara, in tears. She told me that she was contemplating retirement as she was planning to have another child. This was a bolt from the blue for me and I became quite emotional myself.

'I want to help you find another partner, Sania, because I'll be retiring at the end of the year,' said Cara, in tears. We had developed a close bond over the last few months and it was with mixed feelings that our partnership was coming to an end. I wished her well in her efforts to expand her family and we resolved to make our last few tournaments count.

36

THE ROAD TO NO. 1

THE FOCUS HAD to shift to the 2014 Asian games but playing the quadrennial event was turning out to be a tricky balancing act. I was on the cusp of making my first year-end WTA finals, the dream of every professional tennis player, and I was also defending points in both Tokyo and Beijing. The tournament in Japan had been downgraded to a 470-points event from the 900 that it had carried the year before. Wuhan had been added to the schedule after Tokyo, as a special tribute to former world No. 2 Li Na, who hails from the city, and made into a 900-points bonanza before Beijing, which still carried 1,000 points for the winners. These three tournaments offered big points and were likely to decide who would qualify for the WTA finals to be held in Singapore.

The Asian Games coincided with the Wuhan tournament and that put a huge strain on me in terms of balancing my personal ambition and national duty. I thought about it for several days, even as the top three Indian men – Leander Paes, Somdev Devvarman and Rohan Bopanna – all decided to skip the Asian Games to protect their professional rankings. I fully understood the rationale behind their decision and agreed with it. I decided to follow suit and announced my own intention of playing in the World Ranking tournaments instead of the Asian Games.

However, when I woke up the next morning after a restless night, I couldn't shake off the feeling that it wasn't right to skip the opportunity to win another medal for my country in the Asian Games. Missing the professional tournaments would certainly hurt my world ranking and also take away my best chance of qualifying for the super prestigious year-end championships for the first time in my career. Yet, my heart cried out that playing for India in the Games was what I should be doing, irrespective of the consequences, and it was my heart that finally won over my head.

I called AITA president Anil Khanna and informed him that I had decided to represent India at the Asian Games instead of playing in the WTA tournaments. He could not conceal his delight. He knew how important the year-end championships are for a professional tennis player and recognized the sacrifice I was making in order to represent the country. I would do my best to try and win some medals for India even though the team would be handicapped in the absence of the stalwarts of men's tennis, I promised him.

My opting for the Asian Games was big news in the media and positively galvanized the young and inexperienced tennis team that was preparing to represent the country in Guangzhou. Meanwhile, my father and I tried our best to work out the permutations. It would be a great honour for me, and for India, if I could become the first woman from my country to qualify for the WTA finals and this was my golden, realistic chance after missing out due to partner troubles in the previous year. I had done extremely well in earlier years but had failed to qualify and it just would not feel right if I did not play the championships this year as well.

We figured that if I did well in Tokyo and Beijing, I had a reasonably good chance of securing my place with Cara, in spite of missing Wuhan. So I took the plunge and decided to go ahead and play the Asian Games, risking my qualification into the year-end championships.

Before leaving for the Asian Games, I was honoured to meet Prime Minister Narendra Modi. The newly elected PM had tweeted about my US Open win and I was keen to visit him. I flew to Delhi to pay my respects to the prime minister and he surprised me with his incredible memory as he reminded me of his meeting with my sister ten years ago, when he was the chief minister of Gujarat. He even remembered that she was an upcoming pistol shooter. I was fortunate to meet President Pranab Mukherjee too, on the same day.

Cara and I defended our Tokyo title with reasonable ease. Even though we gained fewer points because of the downgrading of the tournament, it went a long way towards soothing my nerves as I headed into the Asian Games. On the first day of the Games, I got the wonderful news that my spot in the championships was confirmed.

I partnered Saketh Myneni and Prarthna Thombare in the mixed and women's doubles events in an extremely successful outing. We bagged the gold in the mixed and bronze in women's doubles to take my overall medal tally in the Asian Games to eight, the highest haul by any Indian in tennis. It is hard to describe the satisfaction that I felt, especially given the tension that had built up preceding the event. Going into the Asian Games, I had been aware that we had a B-team and felt immense pressure as everyone's hopes seemed to be riding on my shoulders. Saketh and Prarthna both gave me incredible support.

A tennis player gets no respite. We have little time to celebrate even the big wins, such as a gold medal at the Asian Games. I headed straight to Beijing for another successful week. Although we were disappointed at not being able to defend our title, Cara and I finished runners-up with wins over the fifth and seventh-seeded teams.

Then came the big year-end championships – the WTA finals. This was our last event together before Cara's retirement. I was on a high after a Grand Slam win at the US Open, the gold in the Asian Games and outstanding results in Tokyo and Beijing. I felt I had achieved substantial success in the latter half of the year and the unbridled pleasure of winning medals for India made me feel buoyant.

The matches in the WTA finals in Singapore turned out to be absolutely thrilling. In the quarters and semis, we scraped through 12-10 against Raquel Kops-Jones and Abigail Spears and 11-9 against Katarina Srebotnik–Kveta Peschke in super tie-breaks. The matches were as close as any we had ever played and yet we came out triumphant, holding our nerve at the end. After these wins, we felt as though we were destined to win the championships and that the worst was behind us.

The stage was now set for the final, against a team we had lost to several times during the year. Su-Wei Hsieh (with whom I had already sealed my partnership for the year 2015) and Peng Shuai would not be an easy team to beat. We would need to hold our nerve one last time this year in another very tight match, we thought, but we needn't have worried.

Cara and I stepped up beautifully for an extremely satisfying night in front of legends like Martina Navratilova, Chris Evert, Billie Jean King and Wimbledon champion Marion Bartoli, who had all been invited for this very special event.

When the match began, I found myself in sublime form, striking the ball with perfect timing, and Cara was splendid at the net as well. I played an absolute cracker of a match, perhaps one of my best, as we broke the record for the least number of games conceded while winning the WTA finals.

I had bagged the biggest title of them all – the 'mother of all Grand Slams' as it is often referred to on the tour. Every team and every player wants to win the WTA finals, which is truly a world championship. The win was a huge impetus on my road to the top, separating me from the rest. It reinforced my belief that the No. 1 spot was mine for the taking.

37

ON TOP OF THE WORLD

I'D HAD A great finish to the year and when I began my 2015 season in January with Su-Wei Hsieh in Brisbane, I felt confident that I had a very good chance of achieving my goal of becoming No. 1 in the world in women's doubles. My partner from Taipei, like me, preferred to play on the deuce court in doubles but her coach, Paul McNamee, was confident that since she possessed razor-sharp reflexes and special volleying skills, it would make no difference at all to her effectiveness if she played on the ad court to accommodate me. He knew that my forehand was my biggest strength.

We started pretty well, reaching the semi-finals in the first tournament of the year, and when we led 6-0 in the super tie-break in the last-four stage against Katarina Srebotnik and Caroline Garcia, a title at the very start of the year seemed a distinct possibility. But we lost the semi-final from an almost unassailable position and that was disheartening. Su-Wei seemed to suddenly freeze when we were on the threshold of victory. But then, this was just the first tournament we were playing together and we needed to get used to each other's game.

Su-Wei, though, was now off to play the qualifying rounds of the Australian Open. So I partnered Bethanie Mattek-Sands in Sydney and struck gold immediately. Beth and I combined beautifully and won the title with consummate ease. Significantly, we beat Martina Hingis and Flavia Pennetta rather easily on the way to the final.

I had pinned a lot of hopes on continuing that great start to the season, when Su-Wei and I came together again for the first Grand Slam of the year in Melbourne. However, we were bundled out in the second round itself by the unheralded team of Alicja Rosolska and Gabriela Dabrowski. It was a very disappointing loss and I was beginning to get the feeling that maybe Su-Wei and I were not going to make a great team despite all our expectations.

After the Australian Open defeat, Su-Wei came up to me and said, 'Sania, I know you are very close to the No. 1 spot in the world and the pressure is getting to me. I just feel that I'm letting you down.'

'We'll do better in the next tournament,' I comforted her with a smile.

But that was not to be. We lost the first round to Alla Kudryavtseva and Anastasia Pavlyuchenkova in Dubai and Su-Wei was distraught after that loss. She suggested that I needed to find someone else as my partner since she was struggling. She also believed that she was uncomfortable playing in the ad court and according to her that was another reason for me to look for a different partner.

I came across Martina Hingis in the players' locker room and suggested to her that since she too was struggling a bit (she had lost the first round in Dubai), we could perhaps think in terms of a partnership. Martina seemed to be interested. Later that night, both of us had a long, candid conversation in my room. We discussed tennis, our future plans and some of our goals. We then decided to wait for another week. We would play the next tournament with our original partners and then take a call on our future together.

In Doha, Su-Wei insisted that since this could be the last tournament that we were playing together, she would like to play on the forehand court. She felt she would be of more use from that side. I agreed to play on the backhand side.

We had a pretty good tournament in Doha and, in fact, did not lose a set until the final. Su-Wei was playing much better from the deuce court and I played just about well enough to continue to win despite playing on my 'wrong' side. However, in the final, we lost to the American team of Raquel Kops-Jones and Abigail Spears and had to settle for the runners-up trophy.

It had been an inspired performance to reach the final under the circumstances and I felt hopeful about our partnership now. This was my first tournament as an ad court player and I had managed to hold my own even though we had lost to a team that Bethanie and I had beaten in the Sydney final. Su-Wei looked quite comfortable on the deuce court and things could only improve from here.

Martina had followed my progress to the final in Doha and she too thought that having done well, I would not consider changing my partner. But we needed to decide quickly. I spoke to my father about the options and he was quite adamant that, at that point, Martina was the right choice for me. He was back home on a break from the circuit but spent the night watching the recording of the Doha final and all the other earlier round matches that Su-Wei and I had won. He called me early the next morning and gave me his verdict.

'I know you are pretty good while playing from the ad court, Sania, but you negate the strength of your forehand, which is easily the best part of your game,' he said. 'If you want to become the No. 1 doubles player in the world, you will need to play on the deuce court. Martina is perfect for you as she's a master of the ad court and knows what it is to be a champion.'

When the year began, Martina and I were nowhere on each other's radar as far as partnering on court was concerned. Yet, circumstances contrived to bring us together as a team and by end-February we had struck a deal to play together. We would begin with the American swing of the circuit and then take a call on the future, depending on how we performed.

The Martina–Sania phenomenon was getting ready to take the tennis world by storm!

*

Martina and I had an incredibly dominant start, winning the prestigious Indian Wells and Miami tournaments without dropping a set. In both the finals we defeated my ex-partner Elena Vesnina and Ekaterina Makarova, who at that point were the biggest threats to my being crowned No. 1. With these two titles in my bag, I was even closer to achieving my dream.

The next tournament was in Charleston, South Carolina. We had initially not planned on competing there. However, as things stood, if we played and won in Charleston, I would take over from the Italians, Sara Errani and Roberta Vinci, as the No. 1 player in the world. Martina was more than willing to play with me for the fifth week in a row to help me achieve my goal as soon as possible.

We were both exhausted by the time we reached the tournament site in the sleepy town of South Carolina. I was very keen to win the title and earn the coveted top spot. It would take the monkey off my back. The fact that Martina agreed to continue playing despite a long month on the road increased the respect that I had for her as a person and brought us closer to each other in our young partnership. She knew what it meant to be No. 1. 'I'll be there if you want to play,' she had said.

After having won in Indian Wells and Miami on hard courts, we needed to quickly make the adjustment to the unique green clay of Charleston and to the different balls that were used there. We won the first three rounds in very close matches via the super tie-break and even saved match points in our second round encounter against defending champions Yaraslova Shvedova and Anabel Medina Garrigues. All our opponents knew exactly why we were there. As professional athletes and competitors, we not only vie to create our own records, but also feel duty-bound to make it as difficult as possible for others to beat us on their way to achieving a landmark. It was that competitive spirit that showed in each of the teams we played against. No one wanted to give it to me on a platter and that added to the pressure on us, knowing as we did that we needed to win the title for me to attain the top spot.

All our matches were played late at night and by the time we got to sleep, it was invariably two in the morning. It takes a while for the adrenaline to subside after the excitement of a match and it's only after a few hours that one is able to wind down and fall asleep. The semi-final finished even later than the earlier rounds, just before midnight on Saturday. We would have a good six hours to recover and maybe get a warm-up hit around 1 p.m. before the final that would be played late in the afternoon. Or so we thought.

To our surprise, the final was scheduled for 10.30 a.m. This was tricky. Our body clocks had got accustomed to late mornings and now I had to play the biggest final of my life, with the highest stakes ever, within a few hours of the semi-final and with inadequate sleep. It turned out that since I was in with a chance of achieving the No. 1 ranking, the organizers were keen to time the final to allow maximum viewership of the match on television all around the world. I was under pressure to get to sleep early. We needed to be ready to hit no later than 9 a.m. But even with the mild sedation caused by the allergy pills I was taking at the time, which usually knock one out, I could barely sleep. I must have woken up twenty times during that disturbed night.

We had pushed our practice session back as late as we could, to allow for a few extra minutes of sleep. As a result, we barely had time to change after the warm-up before walking out to the court for the final. This was unusual, as normally we would have around an hour between the warm-up and the match.

Our opponents in our third consecutive final together were Darija Jurak and Casey Dellacqua. I was nervous, but having a legend like Martina by my side was reassuring. As I walked onto the court, I could feel my nerves settling.

We played inspired tennis in the first set and won 6-0 and then took a commanding lead in the second as well before nerves started to get the better of me. It's not every day that you get an opportunity to officially become the best in the universe at anything. With nothing to lose, Jurak and Casey suddenly started to play brilliantly and the game tightened up. I was serving for the title at 5-3 and was broken for the first time in the match, with Martina hitting into the net. She looked back apologetically and I said with a nervous smile, 'It's okay!'

Casey was now serving at 4-5 and I felt wobbly on my feet. I wanted Martina to take every ball and win the match for me from here. I remember praying as Casey prepared to serve to me on match-point. 'Will I manage to put the ball back?' I wondered.

I needn't have worried as Casey served a double fault and handed the match to us! I felt a sense of jubilation and intense relief. It was a deeply emotional moment. Dad, who had been working with me as my full-time coach for the last few years, and his classmate from university, Navin Uncle, were in the players' box, screaming with delight. The WTA organized a cake for a special function on court, to mark and celebrate my new ranking as the No. 1 women's doubles player in the world.

And thus, history was made by a girl from the unlikely city of Hyderabad, who had been teased almost two decades ago for daring to follow in the footsteps of a superstar called Martina Hingis. Fittingly, her partner at this incredible moment in her career was none other than Martina Hingis!

*

Back home for a few days, I joined the Indian Fed Cup team as captain and on the last day of the event, celebrated with my family, close friends and well-wishers. Some of my Bollywood and Tollywood friends joined in, as did a host of celebrities from other sports to make it a memorable occasion. 'Just Turned One' is how my sister Anam christened the party organized by AITA and my family at the beautiful Taj Falaknuma Palace, to commemorate my achievement.

Shoaib had flown down to join us for a few days and touched everyone's heart with a speech that was not just an ode from a husband to his wife, but also from one athlete to another.

Good evening, ladies and gentlemen.
We are here to celebrate Sania 'turning one', which is a very special moment for me ... because this moment has been a part of our dreams together.

And it so happens that Sania made the dream come true on the exact same day as our fifth wedding anniversary. *Ab kis muhn se anniversary gift mangey koi husband?* (Now I can't even ask her for any other gift!)

Sania has given me something bigger than life itself. In fact, she gave us all something bigger than life five days ago ... and that's the power to make dreams come true. The power to dream a dream worthy to believe in ... to dedicate our days and nights to. Something that scares us and consoles us at the same time.

A dream that ignites passion in you to be the best you can be. Because God knows that the amount of hard work and dedication that is needed to bring the best out of you is not something you can see from the surface. It is deep inside you, a burning desire, and only someone close can really see that fire.

I have seen Sania through her fitness and practice schedules ... day in, day out through the past five years. I have heard her tell me her dreams and what she wants to achieve and how she plans to get there. And then I have seen her walk the talk. I remember she told me once that 'I'm happy to do hard work that gives results, because pain is temporary – victory is forever'.

This occasion also gives us hope. The hope to dream to be the world's No. 1. Sania is a living example of what is possible for tennis in India at a global level, especially for women.

So to Sania, I'm so proud of you, and I will always be your No. 1 fan.

Thank you all and have a great evening.

38

WIMBLEDON CHAMPIONS!

HAVING EARNED MYSELF the top ranking in the world, it was as if a huge weight had been lifted from my shoulders. I could move on now, to the next major goal that I had set for myself at the start of the season in 2015. I wanted to win a Grand Slam in women's doubles to prove to myself and to the world that I truly deserved to be the No. 1 player. I already had three Grand Slam trophies in mixed doubles at the US Open, Roland Garros and the Australian Open, but I was yet to win one in women's doubles. Also, a title at Wimbledon had eluded me so far.

Martina and I had enjoyed only modest success in the clay court season compared to our sensational exploits on the hard courts of USA earlier in the year. A final in Rome, a semi-final in Madrid and a quarter-final loss to Lucie Safarova and Bethanie Mattek-Sands in the French Open was what we had to show for our efforts on clay. We had played just one tournament together on grass before Wimbledon and lost in the semis at Eastbourne to Katarina Srebotnik and Caroline Garcia. We needed to step it up for what is regarded by many (including me) as the greatest tennis tournament in the world – Wimbledon! Martina has always loved the grass and I too have found it to my liking, though hard court remains my favourite surface.

The first round was tricky although the score-line of 6-2, 6-2 in our favour was not quite indicative of the competitive nature of the match. We played Saisai Zheng of China and Zarina Diyas of Kazakhstan and they really did test us. We had to use our doubles skills in full measure in order to push the charged duo back and I believe Saisai admitted to her coach later that they had played their best and yet were unable to make a dent in our game.

The next couple of rounds proved to be easier as we outplayed veteran Japanese player Kimiko Date-Krumm and Italian Francesca Schiavone and then went on to outhit the sixteenth-seeded Spanish team of Anabel Medina Garrigues and Arantxa Parra Santonja, who were never comfortable on grass. We were now in the quarter-finals and at the business end of the championships.

We were pitted against the ninth seeds, Yaroslava Shvedova and Casey Dellacqua. We had beaten them earlier on the green clay of Charleston, although we'd had to save match points on that occasion. On the grass of Wimbledon, the four of us played an outstanding match but Martina and I held on for a 7-5, 6-3 win. I was being cheered on among others by my dear friend, Farah Khan, the renowned Bollywood director, who had come down specially to watch me play. It was her first experience of Wimbledon and I could see the pride on her face as she enjoyed every moment.

In the semi-finals, we faced the all-American team of Raquel Kops-Jones and Abigail Spears. We had beaten them before but were initially apprehensive considering that grass happens to be their favourite surface. However, Martina and I came out firing on all cylinders at Wimbledon that day and virtually annihilated our opponents 6-1, 6-2.

Elena Vesnina and Ekaterina Makarova had run through the other half of the draw and earned the right to challenge us for the most prestigious trophy in the world of tennis. They had overcome a 1-5 deficit in the third set in the quarter-finals against Cara Black and Lisa Raymond to get the better of the seasoned duo and looked like a formidable team. They seemed to have gotten over their worst moment of the tournament when they were on the verge of losing in the quarter-finals and seemed to have gained in confidence. We had beaten them twice in the finals of Indian Wells and Miami but grass was going to be different. Their big serves and Makarova's powerful baseline strokes would be more difficult to handle on the Wimbledon greens where the ball tends to skid through.

Generally speaking, I am a very confident person and don't suffer from nerves but the night before the big final, I could barely sleep. I was nervous and edgy and tossed and turned in bed. This was not any other match that I was going to play that Saturday evening. This was the Wimbledon final – the real thing! Millions of kids and aspiring tennis players and even professionals would have dreamed of playing in a final here and I had actually earned myself a shot at winning the trophy. My first final in the home of tennis – and with the whole world watching! I may or may not get the opportunity to play in another final at Wimbledon, I thought. This could well be my only chance to win.

We went to the Wimbledon Park and warmed up on Court 15. I was not feeling the ball as well as I normally do and was mishitting a lot. My father could see that there was something amiss and he understood what it was. I was not my normal confident self, although I tried hard not to show it or even admit it to myself. 'You'll get your timing right once the match starts,' Dad said with a reassuring smile.

Actor and friend Farhan Akhtar was waiting in the lounge along with his father, Javed Akhtar, and his family. I had invited them to watch the match from the players' box. There was tension in the air while we waited for our match to begin and Martina's agent, David Tosas, and my father tried hard to lighten the mood. And then it was time to go to the locker room to ready myself for the biggest match of my life. The time had finally come and the moment of reckoning was now!

When the final began, it took me a while to overcome my nerves. Martina was the only one among the four finalists who had won on this stage before and it showed in the manner in which she started off and held our team together in the initial part of the first set. She looked comfortable. But then Vesnina, who had played a handful of finals at Wimbledon without having won any, seemed to decide that this was to be her big year: she was playing superb, aggressive tennis.

By the end of the fourth game of the match, I felt a lot more relaxed and had found my timing and rhythm, just as my father had predicted. The match was now even and the tension mounted with the crowd getting more and more involved. The level of tennis in that doubles final was unbelievably high and the margin of error was small. At 5-all, Martina's serve was broken and the Russians held in the next game to pocket the first set.

We raised our game in the second set even higher but so did Makarova and Vesnina. There was not a single service break in the second set and we lifted ourselves to win the tie-breaker at 7-4. I played a brilliant set point that seemed to shift the momentum. Vesnina served to me and I hit four strong cross-courts before going down the line and passing Makarova with a forehand winner that was placed to perfection. At one set all, there was little to choose between the two teams. The one that held its nerve would win.

Vesnina was now playing the best tennis of her life. She served and returned well and was all over the net on the volleys. Just a couple of errors on our part and we found ourselves on the verge of elimination. We went down 1-4 in the decider after Martina was broken at love in the fourth game. Then, at two games to five in the final set, we were looking down a deep hole and knew we needed to draw on our inner strength. The Russians were only a game away from crowning themselves with glory but Martina and I kept reminding each other that we were just one service break down and if we could somehow get that back, we were still in the fight. I remember telling her, 'This is what we have worked for all our lives. What's the worst that can happen?'

Martina replied, 'Yes, but I don't want to lose the final.'

I said, 'Me too. But we have arrived where we wanted to. Let's try and enjoy our fight.' And we both smiled. Anybody watching us would have found it strange that we could be so jovial while on the brink of defeat but what probably helped us was that we chose to enjoy the moment. Our day in the sun.

That's when we played some truly inspired tennis. Martina held confidently for 3-5 and then we broke Makarova to get back on serve with my partner flying through the air to finish off a volley at the net on game point. It was getting dark and more and more difficult to see the ball. Martina kept reminding the chair umpire to turn on the lights, but for some reason he didn't agree. The 'hawk eye' which is the computer imaging technology used in tournaments to arbitrate on very tight line calls had to be switched off as the light was not good enough for the computers to function efficiently. 'If even the computers can't see in this light, how do you expect us to see the ball and play a Wimbledon final?' screamed a frustrated Martina, now at her wit's end.

I held my serve for 5-all with a remarkably angled running backhand cross-court winner at game point and then the chair umpire finally decided that it was time to cover the roof of the Centre Court and turn on the lights. The match had suddenly turned around on its head and we marched off to the green room to await the covering of the roof before we could restart. The break had come at a time when the momentum had shifted completely in our favour. Would we able to go back and take control of the match? My father, as our coach, was escorted into our room as per the rules while the Russian coach went in to advise Makarova and Vesnina in their den.

'This has been an unbelievable final and you both should be proud of the way you have fought back so gallantly, girls. Irrespective of what happens in the rest of the match, nobody can take this away from you,' my father said to us as we quickly re-grouped in our little room with the help of some 'rubbing' on our feet from the physiotherapists. 'Now, from here it's anybody's match but we need to play to our strengths to give ourselves the best chance to win. We have to stay aggressive. Sania, when you see a short ball, go for it with all your power and the moment she hits a deep ball, Martina, you have to take your chances and move at the net. It's possible we may still lose but even if we do, we would have gone down while doing the right things.'

When we came out after the break, the applause from the crowds was deafening. The covered roof and the bright lights added to the fantastic atmosphere and the voices of the screaming spectators echoed and resonated. 'This is incredible. I have goosebumps,' I admitted to my partner as we walked towards our half of the court to resume the final. 'Me, too,' Martina said, smiling back at me.

As I turned around and caught a glimpse of our opponents, they appeared a pale shadow of their earlier selves. Their demeanour had changed dramatically and the two teams were a stark contrast. We were smiling and walking almost with a swagger, proud to present ourselves after a thrilling game so far. We had been close to getting knocked out but had clawed our way back to 5-all. One look at Vesnina and Makarova and it was clear that they felt they should have already won and should have been holding the trophy by now. They looked disheartened and the break had certainly not helped them.

We knew it was now a question of playing inspired tennis for ten more minutes and we could end up on top. Vesnina was to serve first and all I could think of at that moment was that I was not going to miss my return. I needed to get the ball back at all costs. We started brilliantly and broke the Russian's serve with some superb strokes. I remember playing an unbelievable backhand down-the-line winner and then Martina hit a beautiful inside-out forehand cross-court that left a hapless Makarova gasping and sealed the most crucial break of the championships.

Martina now had the opportunity to close out the match and at 40-30, game, set and championship point, she pushed in a nervous 65 mph service to Vesnina's backhand. The Russian hit it tamely into the net while attempting to send it down the line. We had won! My partner and I jumped around the Wimbledon Centre Court like schoolgirls, hugging each other, and the crowd, which had supported us all through the match, seemed delirious.

We waved excitedly at our box where I saw my father being congratulated by all those who had watched the final with him. There was David Tosas, of course, and Farhan and his family, Bollywood actress Huma Qureishi, V. Chamundeshwaranath, the former South Zone cricketer, my friend Ebba and her cricketer husband, Azhar

Mahmood. It is strange how at such moments, one notices the most minute details. I saw my father nibbling on a date. It was the month of Ramadan and he would later tell me how it was nearing 'iftar' time when Martina was serving for the match and he held a date in his hand and prayed for my success and just when my historic victory was accomplished at Wimbledon, it was also the precise prescribed time for him to break his fast!

Of course, celebrations would have begun instantly back home in India even as Martina and I went up to the Royal Box to collect our trophies. This was the moment I had waited for all my life! Watching the champions go up to the Royal Box at Wimbledon to proudly receive their trophies was an image that had been imprinted on my mind since I was a little girl. It had provided the inspiration for me to work hard and achieve what I had finally done.

By winning the title here, I had now won in all the four Grand Slam centres of the world to complete my set of trophies. Significantly, I had also scored my first victory in women's doubles. That this should happen in Wimbledon made it all the more special, a dream come true!

39

FLYING HIGH

After the high of my first Wimbledon title in the professional category, it was never going to be easy to re-focus. Martina herself, having won at the 'home of tennis' after seventeen long years, was feeling the strain. It was not just the win that took its toll on us but the way in which the victory had been achieved. We had won on the biggest stage in the world, turning defeat into victory, and found it hard to concentrate and dig deep in the WTA tournaments in Canada and USA that followed Wimbledon after a very short break. We lost in the semis at Toronto and Cincinnati and our supporters were beginning to wonder if we would struggle at the US Open even though we had produced some magic on the American hard courts earlier in the year.

During the weeks leading up to the US Open, I was delighted to get the news that I had been selected to receive the Rajiv Gandhi Khel Ratna Award for the year from the President of India. This is the highest award for a sportsperson in our country and I was thrilled. This was official recognition of my achievements in my profession and I wanted to make sure I received the award myself from President Pranab Mukherjee. This meant that I would have to skip the New Haven tournament and fly back to India from Cincinnati. Immediately after receiving the Khel Ratna at a glittering ceremony at the Rashtrapati Bhavan, I flew back the same night to New York for the US Open, which was to begin in a day.

Perhaps I was risking fatigue from the long travel to and from New Delhi and this could negatively affect my chances at the Grand Slam but I would not have missed the honour of receiving the award from the President for anything in the world. I did ask the organizers in New York for a delayed start and they willingly obliged.

When the last Grand Slam of the year kicked off, we struck form almost immediately. Maybe we had needed a big challenge to fire us up and a Grand Slam is as big as it gets. We lost a total of just eight games in the first three matches and seemed to be gelling really well. Then, quite unexpectedly, we found ourselves 0-5 down in the quarter-finals against the ninth-seeded Chan sisters of Taipei, whom we had lost to in Cincinnati as well. The spectator seats on the northern and southern sides of the Grandstand court, behind the baseline, are a bit lower than is normally the case and we struggled initially to sight the ball early against the stands. However, once we had made the adjustment, we ran through our opponents after turning things around in the first set tie-breaker.

Meanwhile, Flavia Pennetta was having the tournament of her life in singles as well as in doubles. We played the Italian combination of two former World No. 1s, Flavia and Sara Errani, in the semi-finals and the match started off with both teams unwilling to give an inch. Watched by my uncle, Talat Aziz, the ghazal singer, I struck a purple patch at around 3-all in the first set and the match suddenly became one-sided. We won 6-4, 6-1 from there and triumphantly marched into the finals of yet another Grand Slam.

Talat Uncle had lived with Dad and my grandparents in Mumbai when he first came to the city of dreams to earn a name for himself as a ghazal singer. He was now on a musical tour of USA along with Asha Bhonsle and wanted me to meet the legendary singer, who apparently followed my tennis. There was a gap of four days before the final and I accompanied my father and uncle to meet the famed singer at her hotel. I was delighted to learn that not only had she been following tennis from the Bjorn Borg days, but she had also been an ardent fan of cricket for over thirty years.

'It took me more than seven decades to earn this name and fame, Sania, but you are so young and you are already so famous,' she told me, charmingly.

Martina and I still had an unfinished job on hand. We needed to win the final. Yaroslava Shvedova and Casey Dellacqua had reached the final from the other half of the draw and this would be our third meeting with them in the year. I had won the mixed doubles title at Flushing Meadows in 2014. Could I follow up that performance with a victory in the women's doubles at the US Open this year? Besides, Martina and I now had a shot at winning back-to-back Grand Slams, having already bagged the coveted Wimbledon silverware just two months earlier.

The final turned out to be almost one-sided. Martina and I were in immaculate form and beat the Kazakh–Aussie pair 6-3, 6-3 to assert our supremacy in the world of women's doubles. Amazingly, we had not dropped a set and had, in fact, lost a meagre twenty-six games in the entire tournament.

I rushed home hours after receiving the fifth Grand Slam winner's trophy of my career to attend my sister Anam's engagement. Anam is the only sibling I have been blessed with and we are as close as sisters can be. She is about seven years younger to me and I enjoy mothering her, though we also share a lot of each other's secrets. For a very brief period, tennis went on the backburner as I immersed myself in the festivities around her engagement.

Days later, I was back on tour – this time on my way to China for three tournaments that I was scheduled to play in. On the flight to Guangzhou, I felt this immense satisfaction, deep down, at my performances in the year so far. Having captured the Wimbledon and US Open trophies apart from title wins in Sydney, Indian Wells, Miami and Charleston, and having achieved a ranking of No. 1, this was already the most successful year of my career. Of course, there were a few more tournaments to play, but whatever else I could achieve would only be the 'icing on the cake' which I had already baked for myself!

As it transpired, the rest of the season proved to be more than mere 'icing' and the team of 'Santina' (as we now called ourselves) continued to rock the world of women's doubles in a manner that few combinations have ever done in tennis. We swept all the three tournaments in China (Guangzhou, Wuhan and Beijing) and then I went on to defend my year-end finals in Singapore, which I had won in 2014 with Cara Black as my partner. Amazingly, Martina and I did not lose a single set in the championships.

It was a proud moment to be awarded the trophy for being the Year-end No. 1 Team for 2015 and then to justify that status with a comprehensive win in the final, two days later, against Spaniards Garbine Muguruza and Carla Navarro, two leading singles players of the day, whose extraordinary skills had seen them rise during the year to great heights in doubles as well. The legendary Martina Navratilova had seen me play the final of a lifetime at the same event a year ago and it was she who handed us the WTA trophy again. Her generous comment about my 'awesome' effort against the Spanish team made my day – no, year! To be acknowledged by one of the greatest tennis players of all time was an honour as significant as any of the trophies that had come my way.

My tenth title since January and that, too, in the super prestigious WTA finals was a fitting end to an unbelievable year. I had achieved virtually everything in this sport that I had ever thought I was capable of doing. I felt truly blessed. With the number of wins Martina and I had racked up in the last seven months, it was easy to feel invincible. After the US Open, I had received a text message from a dear friend: 'There will be many times that you could be No. 1, but few moments when you will feel invincible. Enjoy this moment!' I thought our blitzkrieg through the last Grand Slam of 2015 was aptly described by this message.

Martina and I did not feel as though we could lose. We ran through the competition. As an athlete, there are not many times when you feel like this. Winning after being 2-5 down in the third set of the Wimbledon final was a big turning point for us. Had we lost there,

I feel that Martina and I would not have been able to stamp our authority the way we did at the US Open and in the tournaments we won towards the end of the year after that win. From there on, we were the best team on the circuit by a mile.

Having said that, my years on the tour have taught me not to get ahead of myself, ever. Martina and I were expected to win every match that we played but teams also came out swinging harder at us. We were privileged to be the 'hunted' pair, with others having to deal with the problem of trying to break our momentum. But we also knew that we had to bring our 'A' game on to win every match we played and even without it we still needed to find a way to win. The difference between the No. 1 and No. 10 ranked teams in tennis is usually very small. So there is no room for arrogance whatsoever. Our losses would now be more talked about than our wins and that would add considerable pressure.

Martina and I knew we simply could not afford to be complacent. We both strive for perfection and are never fully satisfied with our wins. We almost invariably find ourselves discussing details of what we could have done better. That, perhaps, has been the key to our success together over a prolonged period of time.

The winning streak continued into the year 2016 as well, as Martina and I not only won in Brisbane (where she was defending her previous year's title) and in Sydney (where I was defending mine) but went on to add our third consecutive Grand Slam title after a stupendous run-up to the Australian Open. The final in Sydney against Kristina Mladenovic and Caroline Garcia was a memorable one where we came back from a set and 2-5 down to win after a sensational turnaround. This match made us believe that losing was no longer an option, at least in the immediate future!

Then at the Australian Open, we lost just one set in the entire tournament and that was in the quarter-final against the big-serving Coco Vandeweghe of USA and Anna-Lena Groenefeld of Germany. In the semis we ran away with a 6-1, 6-0 win over Czech Karolina Pliskova and Julia Goerges of Germany. The final was a fiercely fought encounter as we confronted the top Czech team of Andrea Hlavackova and Lucie Hradecka, against whom I had lost a Grand Slam final with Elena Vesnina as my partner in the French Open in 2011. It was time to settle an old score and Martina and I combined to do just that!

With Andrea starting brilliantly, we struggled a bit in the first set before stepping it up in the tie-break, which we won easily. Once we were ahead, the match eased up in our favour and we won comfortably to pocket my sixth career Grand Slam title (including the mixed) and third in a row in women's doubles.

A fortnight later, we won our ninth consecutive title in the Russian city of St Petersburg and the streak finally ended in Doha after we had extended our run to forty-one victories in a row. This is a unique record under the new no-ad, deciding point and super tie-break rules that have been formulated into the doubles game and is one which will take a long time to be beaten.

The twelve-month period that began with the Indian Wells tournament in March 2015 and ended with Doha in February 2016 had brought Santina as many as thirteen titles including Wimbledon, the US Open, the Australian Open and the year-end WTA finals. This was undoubtedly the most successful period of my career.

40

A BLESSED LIFE

LIFE AS A professional tennis player was never a bed of roses for me and yet I would not exchange it for any other. I missed out on a lot of time with my family. I have lived my life out of suitcases, unable to cultivate lasting friendships or even relationships. Constant scrutiny of the kind that I have been exposed to and the pressure of unrealistic expectations to perform at the highest level, day in and day out, have not been easy to handle. Over the last two decades, I have paid a heavy price for my passion but tennis has also given me fame, respect, honour, a satisfying career, and a lot more in life. I cannot thank the Almighty enough.

Along with success came recognition and I was privileged to be honoured with the Arjuna Award in 2004 and the Padma Shri in 2006 when I was still a teenager. Ten years later, I was awarded the Padma Bhushan in 2016. Being considered worthy of the Rajiv Gandhi Khel Ratna is the ultimate dream of any Indian sportsperson and I consider myself very fortunate to have been chosen for this privilege. Over the years, dozens of organizations and institutions have chosen to honour me with different accolades, including the 'Daughter of the Soil' citation – all of which was a truly humbling experience for me even at that young age. To be conferred with an honorary doctorate by MGR University, Chennai was absolutely amazing.

The chief minister of Andhra Pradesh, Chandrababu Naidu,

presented me with a citation embossed on wood for bringing honour to the state and country. Today it adorns a wall in my trophy room. Shri Surjit Singh Barnala, who was the governor of my state when I came home triumphantly with the Junior Wimbledon trophy, wrote me a touching, emotional letter at the time of my wedding, about how he had always looked upon me as his own daughter. He is an artist and presented me with a self-painted canvas of a scenery that hangs proudly in my home.

I was fortunate to have admirers from various countries of the world, who enjoyed the way I played and the manner in which I struck the tennis ball. However, as is only to be expected, my biggest following has come from amongst my own countrymen. Indians are amazing people. We make up almost 20 per cent of the world's population and you cannot argue with numbers.

My fellow countrymen were there to cheer me on, not only in India but in almost every venue that I played at, anywhere in the world, and they took a lot of pride in my very presence at these international events. Their happy smiles whenever I won egged me on and the dozens of mails that I've received from fans on a daily basis for years have been a source of joy and encouragement and acted as a tonic to spur me on. Unfortunately, due to my relentless professional commitments and paucity of time, it has not been physically possible to reply to most of them.

There were also a few letters that moved me and sometimes brought tears to my eyes. One such letter was written by a young boy who was suffering from terminal cancer and had only a few months to live. He wrote that he was my greatest fan and that he knew he was destined to die soon. He had just one last wish – to receive a personally autographed photograph from me before the end of his short life. I sent it to him instantly and prayed for him.

There was another emotionally charged letter that I received from a retired Indian Army officer, who addressed me as his granddaughter and enclosed a cheque for five hundred rupees in the envelope. He said that he was an army man who had spent his life serving our country but now he was retired and old. In all his life, he had not imagined that an Indian sports woman would give him the joy and sense of pride that I had given him with my attacking brand of tennis. He wrote that he was certain I would have earned a lot of money already as a successful tennis player but here was a cheque for five hundred rupees from a proud and grateful grandfather of modest means, to show his appreciation for the dignity that I had brought to our country. I never encashed that cheque.

It was tennis that provided me with the great privilege of meeting former Prime Minister Manmohan Singh at his residence in New Delhi and former President A.P.J. Abdul Kalam at Rashtrapati Bhavan. I also had the honour of meeting former President Pratibha Patil at a banquet in New Delhi. More recently, I was honoured to meet Prime Minister Narendra Modi and President Pranab Mukherjee as well. Spending time with these luminaries was precious, truly inspiring and an education in itself.

I have featured in cover stories of dozens of highly respected periodicals in India but I think it took everyone by surprise when I was featured on the cover of an international magazine like *Time*, which also picked me for the 2005 Asian Hero award 'for helping to make our world a better place'. More than a decade later, I was chosen as one of the '100 most influential people in the world' by the same magazine that also listed such political heavyweights as President Vladimir Putin of Russia.

To add to the euphoria, President George W. Bush of the United States of America visited Hyderabad in 2006 on a diplomatic tour. He travelled to New Delhi that same evening and at a massive press conference that was covered worldwide, the American President smiled disarmingly at the crowd of journalists and said, 'I was happy to be in the city of Sania Mirza this morning'!

I believe in destiny and the will of God. There has to be a reason for every little thing that happens in our world. I realized very early in my career that success and public recognition provide a rare opportunity to contribute effectively to social and charity work. This is something I intend to continue to take advantage of.

Soon after I won the girls' doubles title at Wimbledon in 2003, Sushma Swaraj, who was then the Union Minister for Social Welfare, approached me with an offer to work as a brand ambassador for the girl child in the fight against female infanticide and foeticide in India. I was just sixteen years old, but I took my job seriously.

My research on the subject revealed some chilling facts and figures about the dreadful plight of girls in our country. In many parts of India, newborn girls are mercilessly killed and some are destroyed even before their birth in their mother's womb in a savage, inhuman and unforgiveable practice that has been prevalent for far too long.

What is even more surprising and depressing is the fact that girls are killed not only in remote villages but also in metropolitan cities, where people are expected to be better educated and more socially aware. At some of the public meetings I went to in order to spread the message against this ghastly crime, I remember Sushma ji's voice warning the public at large, 'Stop this practice, dear friends, varna dhoondte reh jaoge', meaning that if you don't stop female infanticide and foeticide, the ratio of girls to boys will keep diminishing and you will soon be left 'searching for girls to marry'!

I enjoyed my association with Sushma ji and continued to propagate the cause of the girl child whenever I could, even after my term as brand ambassador had come to an end. I wrote articles against female infanticide and foeticide in my weekly newspaper column and used several other platforms to help improve the state of the girl child in our society. It is a cause that is close to my heart.

Equality for women is another important issue for me and I was privileged to be accorded the opportunity to work in this direction when I was appointed the UN Women's Goodwill Ambassador for South Asia in November 2014. I happened to be the first Indian woman to be given this responsibility.

I also enjoyed working with the SACH Foundation, an initiative by the Apollo Group of Hospitals. The foundation identified several thousand children with a heart problem which, if left untreated, could result in their death within the next six months. The ailment could be easily treated at a heavily discounted cost of Rs 50,000 per patient, thanks to the initiative of SACH, and the child could go on to lead a perfectly healthy and normal life. My job was to spread awareness so that the disease could be more easily diagnosed and also to raise funds for the unwell children so that they could be treated and saved.

When I won a substantial amount with some help from Lara Dutta in Amitabh Bachchan's *Kaun Banega Crorepati* in the special celebrity segment of the popular TV programme, I used the money for SACH and I continue to work with Apollo Hospitals to try and spread the message of good health amongst those who cannot afford it. I can honestly say that work of this nature gives me great satisfaction and I hope to continue doing it long after I have stopped playing tennis. It makes me feel privileged and adds a new meaning to my life.

My family is involved with a charity of our own and once I am through with tennis, I hope to get more actively involved with this work, which my parents are currently engaged in. I cannot thank the Almighty enough for the opportunity He has given me to serve society in my own small way, apart from the gift of millions of blessings that I cannot even begin to count.

I have been extremely fortunate to have achieved what I did in tennis and the game has given me a wonderful, fulfilling life. I feel I owe it to society, my sport and my country to give back what I can. My family and I have learnt so much about international tennis in the last quarter of a century, which would all go to waste if we did not pass on this knowledge to the next few generations of tennis players in our country.

Is it not disappointing that Leander, Mahesh and I are the only three Indian players to have won a Grand Slam title in the history of world tennis? As a country, could we not have done better than producing just three top-30 singles players in Vijay Amritraj, Ramesh Krishnan and myself in the last forty years since the game turned professional? I am determined to improve India's record in this amazing global sport and I hope to take our country forward by at least a few more steps in this pursuit of excellence.

My dream has always been to develop a world-class academy right here in India and to churn out top-level juniors and professional tennis players. This is the kind of facility that I badly missed being able to use while I was developing as a youngster.

And so I set up the Sania Mirza Tennis Academy in my hometown of Hyderabad. I have seen enough on the world stage to understand what a difficult task it is to produce Grand Slam champions. The work will have to start from the grassroots level and I believe I have already started off on the trail to put a professional system in place. I have also formulated a scheme for adopting, supporting and grooming specially talented youngsters from rural India.

We will need to start by producing a bunch of juniors who will compete in the Junior Grand Slams. We will have to support and monitor their progress to ensure that at least a handful of them make it to the top-100 in professional tennis. Towards this end, I will need to create a team that understands what world-class competition is all about in a sport like tennis. I will have to build up support from several quarters. A lot of work needs to be done.

Tennis is a truly global sport with a phenomenally large following in all corners of the world. There have been occasions when the top-10 ranked players all belonged to different countries and the top-60 were representatives of as many as thirty different nations. This is a record that is unlikely to be equalled in any sport apart from tennis, where the next champion can emerge out of virtually any country in the world.

The game has also given successive generations more colourful champions and personalities than perhaps any other sport has done and this has inspired even more countries to embrace it. A great deal of effort and sacrifice goes into producing a professional tennis player. But the respect that a country earns by being represented at mega sporting events like the Grand Slams has to be seen to be believed and experienced to be understood. All I can say is that every drop of sweat and blood shed in the process is worth its weight in gold.

I have always dared to dream because I believe that dreams are the seeds that lead to achievement. However, it is not enough to merely dream. You need to back it up with years of hard work to ultimately produce the result that makes a difference.

My vision for the development of tennis in our country may seem far-fetched but I have been in this position before. When I was a little girl pursuing a dream, nobody believed an Indian woman could win a Grand Slam title or be ranked No. 1 in the world. I have always relished the challenge of defying the odds that are stacked against me. I want to do it at least one more time and play a constructive role in nurturing the next generation of Grand Slam champions from India that our country so richly deserves to have.